# In the
# MeanTime

# In the
# MeanTime

## Celebrating Everyday Wisdom

# William Dunphy

FOREST OF PEACE
Publishing

Suppliers for the Spiritual Pilgrim
Leavenworth, KS

# In the MeanTime

copyright © 2002, by William Dunphy

Library of Congress Cataloging-in-Publication Data

Dunphy, William, 1933-
    In the meantime : celebrating everyday wisdom / William Dunphy.
    p. cm.
    ISBN 0-939516-62-4 (pbk.)
      1. Spiritual Life–Meditations.  I. Title.
    BL624.2 .D88 2002
    242–dc21

                             2002022150

*published by*
Forest of Peace Publishing, Inc.
PO Box 269
Leavenworth, KS 66048-0269  USA
1-800-659-3227
www.forestofpeace.com

*printed by*
Hall Commercial Printing
Topeka, KS 66608-0007

1st printing: March 2002

Dedicated to

## CODY,

MY MENTOR,
MY PLAYMATE,
MY GRANDSON

May he always delight
in everyday wisdom

Special thanks go out to Brad Lowell, editor of the Concordia (Kansas) Blade-Empire. In May of 1996 I handed him, for his approval, three columns I had entitled "In the MeanTime." Thus began a professional and personal relationship I have treasured through the years.

I also thank my beloved wife, Emma. Her patience and encouragement in my quest to be a writer have been a constant inspiration to me.

# Contents

# Introduction
# Stuck in the MeanTime

How often have we heard the expression, "I'm going to do this someday, but in the meantime...." I don't know if you're like me, but I discovered recently that I have spent far too much of my life in the meantime.

Time in the mean too often is time spent waiting for things to happen rather than making things happen. It's "mean" because we feel we have so little, if any, control over it. We are going to fix up our house when we have the money; in the meantime we allow it to deteriorate. Since meantime doesn't hold out much chance for excitement, our lives become a drag. We are going to be happy when we get the right job, when we can buy this house or that product, when we win the lottery. But in the meantime: BLAH. It's the meantime because we don't have the job we desire, material things are out of reach and the lottery numbers never fall right. We feel helpless to do anything about our sorry state. Our meantime is filled with dissatisfaction and unfulfillment.

"Why are you rushing so much?" asked the Rabbi. "I am rushing after my livelihood," the man answered. "And how do you know," said the Rabbi, "that your livelihood is running before you, so that you have to rush after it? Perhaps it's behind you and all you need do is stand still!"

This thought-provoking little story raises some interesting issues. Maybe we are given meantime to evaluate our priorities. What do we really *need* to be happy?

Working at the local animal shelter has given me a real appreciation of these words of Walt Whitman:

> I think I could turn and live with animals, they are so placid and self-contained, I stand and look at them long and long. They do not sweat and whine about their condition. They do not lie awake in the dark and weep

for their sins. They do not make me sick discussing their duty to God. Not one is dissatisfied, not one is demented with the mania of owning things. Not one kneels to another, nor to his kind who lived thousands of years ago. Not one is respectable or unhappy over the whole earth.

As if she knew what I was writing about, our cat, Fluffy, jumped into my lap. Because of a genetic defect, she is completely deaf. Yet I have never seen her sweat or whine about her condition. Life remains an adventure for her despite what we humans have defined as a handicap.

Because it seems to define our present society, one phrase from Walt Whitman especially struck me: "Not one is demented with the mania of owning things." I think we are hard-pressed to really believe that our worth is greater because of what we *are* than because of what we *have*. Our society still measures success by material possessions.

By that measure I would have to admit I fall well short of the mark. In the meantime, I much prefer how Robert Louis Stevenson defines the meaning of success:

That man is a success who has lived well, laughed often and loved much; who has gained the respect of intelligent men and the love of children; who has filled his niche and accomplished his task; who leaves the world better than he found it whether by a perfect poem or a rescued soul; who never lacked appreciation of earth's beauty or failed to express it; who looked for the best in others and gave the best he had.

Success, as well as happiness, is like a butterfly; the more you chase it, the more it will elude you. But if you turn your attention to, and make most important, that which you happen to be doing at the moment, it will come and rest on your shoulder.

It is my hope that you, the reader, will find in these reflections some simple ways to sit still long enough to be a landing pad for butterflies.

## 1

MeanTime Musings

# Beauty and Value in the MeanTime

If the truth were told, all of us who believe in the hereafter are living in the meantime. To complicate matters, we believe that how we conduct ourselves in this meantime will determine our choice when we pass from the here to the after.

I said, "to complicate matters," but in reality it is very simple. If we intend to be content in the after, we will need to learn to be content in the here.

I don't mean "content" in that grin-and-bear-it sort of way that borders on fatalism. Rather, we must learn to be content with who we are and know that the world needs us just as we are. I'd like to repeat some advice I gave to a class of high school seniors way back in 1971:

> I am asking you to always remember that you have a destiny that is completely unique in the eyes of God and the history of humankind. There has never been anyone just like you nor will there ever be again. So be yourself. Others need you just as the Lord has willed you to be. Sure you have faults; all of us are incomplete in some way. Your limitations are an invitation to union with others, a union rooted in love. Have but one desire, to be fully, without reservation, what God wants you to be, and thus you will be what the world needs you to be.

I have always found Charlie Brown to be a good, down-to-earth role model. One of the other characters in the *Peanuts* comic strip, upon finding him building a birdhouse, asked, "How's it coming along, Charlie Brown?" Without embarrassment, Charlie explained, "Well, I'm a lousy carpenter, I can't nail straight, I can't saw straight, and I always split the wood. I'm nervous, I lack confidence, I'm stupid. I have poor taste and absolutely no sense of design.... So, all things considered, it's coming along okay." Charlie was a little hard on himself, but he didn't allow his limitations to prevent him from going ahead with the project.

And, you know what? I'll bet he never heard any complaints from the birds who occupied his birdhouse.

When we pass from the here to the after, our choice will be finalized. Now, in the meantime, we are free to change our mind.

Have you ever thought that some people, given the option, would not choose that state we refer to as heaven. They would simply be bored to death with all that peace, love and happiness. Can you imagine turning on your TV and being able to find only good news? Can you imagine a soap opera in which all the characters are virtuous? In much of our culture that would be a definition of *boring*.

As was often the case, the late, great *Calvin and Hobbes* was able to put this in perspective. In one episode Calvin tries to explain to Hobbes, "Popular culture isn't to blame for selling twisted values. Movies, records and TV shows reflect the reality of our times. Artists depict hatred and violence because that's what they see." Hobbes asks, "Why don't they see things of beauty and value?" Calvin responds, "Because boring stuff doesn't sell." Hobbes says with raised eyes, "Such vision and integrity." Calvin concludes, "There's nothing like a good gunfight to uplift the spirit."

Hobbes' question needs to be answered by each of us in a personal way, "Why don't they see things of beauty and value?" I once heard our society characterized as knowing the price of everything but the value of nothing.

Living in the meantime gives us a chance to sharpen our skills in seeing and recognizing things of beauty and value. Then we will be able to make the proper choice when we pass from the here to the after.

# A Lionhearted Chicken

I was born under the sign of Leo. The symbol of Leo is a lion. Lions are kings, so being born under this sign has made me feel strong and confident. Therefore, I was not at all surprised when my mother informed me that I could trace my ancestry to French nobility.

Then one day a funny thing happened. While eating dinner in a Chinese restaurant, I found out I was born, according to the Chinese calendar, in the year of the chicken. Although chickens do have good qualities, *strong* and *confident* are not usually among them. I was overwhelmed with ambivalent feelings. What was I anyway, a chickenhearted lion or a lionhearted chicken?

This bit of nonessential knowledge introduces a fact of which we are all aware: the natural tension that exists in all of our lives. In this meantime we often find ourselves pulled in different directions. We possess a built-in sense of the proper thing to do. But there is another sense, which also seems to be built-in, that says, "Get real." It's summed up in a poster I have depicting a gorilla lying on his back with his head against a stump. The caption is, "Just when I knew all of life's answers, they changed all the questions."

The struggle I would like to address here comes from a Book I read on a regular basis. It says, "Anyone among you who aspires to greatness must serve the rest, and whoever wants to rank first among you must serve the needs of all." If I didn't have such high regard for this book, I might consider that statement subversive. It certainly doesn't fit into the good old U.S.A. way of doing things. The servant role is usually not on the list of occupations to which people aspire. It is, however, a role more and more must assume today just to survive.

Recently, I was listening to some cassette tapes I had requested at an 800 number. The persons on the tapes were attempting to convince me that I could be a millionaire, in a relatively short time, by setting up my own business in my home, using a computer and their expertise.

As I listened, I kept thinking of that quotation from the book. I wondered if aspiring to be a millionaire would put me at odds with the aspiration to greatness spoken of in the quotation. What better way to "serve the needs of all" than with lots of money. When I think of winning the lottery, my thoughts turn to all the people with whom I could share my winnings. Of course, in my weaker moments, my thoughts stray to seeing myself behind the wheel of a Dodge Viper. As a Leo, I might be drawn to a Cougar or even a Jaguar.

It would be a great thing if concern and generosity toward the needs of others grew in direct proportion to the growth of one's bank account. Unfortunately that doesn't often seem to be the case.

I'm always struck by how often — in the recorded reaction to the winning of money — the phrase "O my God" is heard. Is it just an expression of surprise or our society's Freudian slip as to the role money actually plays in our lives?

Recently I read this comment: "It has been said that poverty is not the real problem in America; the real problem is affluence — rising affluence that brings with it detachment, separation, indifference to the poor." In the Johnson administration we declared war on poverty and lost. Could it be we chose the wrong enemy?

You've just been given a tour through the mind of a lionhearted chicken. Don't be frightened, his roar is much worse than his peck.

# Saturation Point

If you would like to take the time, I have an interesting little exercise for you to begin this reflection. Take half an hour or more if you wish, and simply sit still. No TV! A little mood music may be allowed, but it's not recommended. Find a comfortable place, perhaps a favorite chair. You may even lie down if you promise to stay awake.

For this time I would like you to think about the quality of your life. Quality would have to do with how happy or satisfied you are with your life as it is right now. While you contemplate the quality of your life, take a mental tour of your house and surroundings and think of all the things you own (outright or paying on). Now think of how these material things affect the quality of your life. In what way do they make you happy? Do they help in your relationship with your spouse? Have they brought your family closer together? Which material thing would you find most difficult to live without? Which things do you consider absolutely necessary for your survival? What other things are you anticipating purchasing and why? Enough questions for now, but you may add as many as you wish.

Maybe you can help me in my research. I'm working on a theory which says that, quite possibly, our society has reached the saturation point regarding material things that promise to make things easier for us and thus add to the quality of our lives. In other words, can you think of something that hasn't been invented that you feel would add significantly to the quality of your life?

I see our society exhibiting the same symptoms as those associated with the eating disorder *bulimia*. We have this insatiable appetite for material things. When we no longer have any room for more, we purge the old so we can buy the new and improved.

Just maybe it's time we followed the admonition from one of the Master's parables about the kingdom of God. He said it was like a dragnet thrown into a lake, which collected all sorts of things. "When it was full, they hauled it ashore and sat down to put what was worthwhile into containers. What was useless they threw away."

That's what that little exercise I suggested in the beginning was for. Have we taken the time recently to sit down and examine what we have in our nets — to separate the valuable from the useless? We need to recognize what is excess baggage in our lives and deal with it accordingly. It can be a real drag on our journey.

You may be thinking, "What a killjoy!" Yet there is something about this kind of sorting through our material possessions that frees us for joy. A beautiful meditation from a book of daily meditations for women entitled *Each Day a New Beginning* addresses our real needs: "We get what we need, in the way of relationships, adventures, joys and sorrows, today and every day. Celebrating what we get and knowing there is good in it eases whatever trial we are undergoing. *We are cared for*, right now. We need not lament what we think we need. We do have what we need. We will always get what we need, when we need it.

"(In the meantime) I will breathe deeply and relax. At this moment my every need is being attended to. My life is unfolding exactly as it should."

Of course, the key word in the meditation, repeated seven times, is "need." I guess the whole idea of my little exercise was to get us to thinking about what we really *need* to live a quality life.

# Quiet Time

In the last reflection we talked about values. What is it that we really value? One thing that I value highly is quiet time, time to be with myself with as little distraction as possible. I need to qualify "with myself" a little since much of my quiet time is spent with an uninvited guest to whom I can never say no.

Most often my quiet time is spent in an easy chair with a book in my lap and other books within reach. Also within reach is a cup of coffee. In the morning my coffee is "Perfect Balance." Could anyone ask for more?

Quiet times, in my experience, have to be created. They don't just happen. I am not suggesting we put quiet time ahead of family responsibilities. I do know in my heart, however, that without quiet times my ability to respond to these responsibilities will suffer.

Quiet time is not simply time when you don't have anything else to do. It is not simply passive time but is really quite active time. It's tricky speaking of quiet times being active. We tend to define activity in terms of movement. Snoopy protested when he was accused of doing nothing, lying on his doghouse: "On the contrary, I'm absorbing solar energy."

Personally, I avoid having any agenda for my quiet times. My duty is to show up and absorb whatever is in store for me. Since my quiet times are mostly in the morning, I may take the time to write down a few things I would like to get done that day. Doing it at this time puts the things to be accomplished in their proper perspective. I have been amazed through the years how trivial pursuits often become matters of life and death in our minds. Quiet times bring into focus how few things really matter in life. Quiet times bring into focus what we most value.

The book I have in my lap and those nearby are there in case I need a jump-start. I look at them, or not. I read as much or as little as I need. Sometimes just a sentence, maybe just a word. Words like "wholehearted" and "unreservedly" always interest me. Have I ever done anything wholeheartedly, without reservation? I sometimes feel like Snoopy. Upon being told by Linus to remove his paw from Linus' blanket or suffer the consequences, Snoopy, after removing his paw, thinks to himself, "That's my life, full of unsuffered consequences."

The key to successful quiet times is to expect everything but not be disappointed if nothing happens. Quiet times are for soaking up spiritual energy. We may not feel the results until we really need them.

The late Thomas Merton said, "When we're trying to fix everything and everyone, when we're trying to fix every problem we come across, our busyness destroys the root of inner wisdom that makes our work fruitful." Quiet times reconnect us to that inner wisdom. Acting and giving are not necessarily more useful than resting and receiving.

In case you've been wondering, the uninvited guest in my quiet times is a large white cat. Anyone who may have read my book, *Snooper's Tale*, knows that I love cats. My quiet time cat, Fluffy, is usually not a distraction unless she is in a playful mood. She has taught me the art of stretching before I settle in for my quiet time. Being comfortable physically will add to your spiritual experience. Her presence also helps me keep things in perspective. I often look at her and think of what her day is going to be like. I think that my love for this creature of God is only a shadow of the love God has for me — so of what do I have to be afraid? She's got it made and so do I!

# The Final Freedom

If you don't know by now, you will soon learn that I am addicted to quotations, preferably short and thought-provoking ones. Their source is of little concern if they speak to me and I see the wisdom contained therein. This reflection's offering is from Helen M. Luke:

> We hurry through the so-called boring things in order to attend to that which we deem more important, interesting. Perhaps the final freedom will be a recognition that everything in every moment is "essential" and that nothing at all is "important."

Not only is this quote short and thought provoking, it seems to verify what I've said about the meantime. The present time is "mean" because we are never quite "there." Try this little experiment. You've filled your glass with ice and have poured in your favorite beverage, or you've grabbed an ice-cold can from the frig. You're hot and in need of refreshment. Put your hand around the glass or can and just caress it for a while. Think about what's happening. The millions of cells that make up the sense of touch in your hand are transmitting messages to your brain telling you this is cold. Concentrate, just for a few seconds, on "coldness," not on what you are about to do or where you have to be as soon as you've finished. Try this exercise once, and I expect you will be amazed at the sensations you will feel in your hand. How many "sensational" moments we miss because we are not "there" when they happen to us.

This awareness leads naturally to saying something about our "fast food" society. We treat eating as though it is something to get out of the way so that we can attend to the more important things in our lives. It seems to me, however, that food doesn't like to be treated that way. It likes to be treated with more respect and can rebel in some very painful ways. Of course, we often work to correct that with chemicals that will keep food in its place.

A *Course in Miracles* says,

> The only aspect of time that is eternal is *now*.... *Now* is the closest approximation of eternity that this world offers. It is in the reality of now, without past or future, that the beginning of the appreciation of eternity lies.

I have told people that if they wished to know what heaven is like they should take an ecstatic moment and think of how it would be if it lasted forever. The problem with that exercise is that in our fast-paced world we don't have time to have ecstatic moments — and if we had one we probably wouldn't recognize it.

Another quotation, from Thich Nhat Hanh:

> From time to time, to remind ourselves to relax, to be peaceful, we may wish to set aside some time for a retreat, when we can walk slowly, smile, drink tea with friends, enjoy being together as if we are the happiest people in the world.

The word retreat is most appropriate to what we have been talking about. In this case our retreat would be from the front lines in order to regroup. We do this in order to see if the strategy we have been using is really working. Unfortunately, most vacations would not be classified as retreats. They may involve a change in our daily activities, but the pace usually remains the same.

Are we "peaceful" people? Do we "enjoy being together"? Or is it always necessary that we be "doing" together? The commercials of the soft drink whose last name rhymes with "do" try to convince us that the more active we are the happier we will be. Unfortunately, I must admit they have pretty well succeeded.

# Is Time More Valuable Than You?

**Who cares!!!** What would your reaction be if you saw those words on the face of every clock you looked at? Recently, I received an advertisement for such a timepiece. All the numerals are in a heap at the bottom, and those two words are emblazoned across the middle. It's touted as a great gift for a happy retiree or anyone who could benefit from taking life at a more relaxed pace. The advertisement does assure us, however, that its quartz movement provides ever-accurate readings.

Since I have chosen to use the word "time" in the title of this book, I feel it's a topic worthy of pursuing. Contributing to the ad was an article entitled "Timeless Wisdom" from the very first issue of *Spirituality and Health* magazine. A subtitle for this article read, "Why a clock is never in the present but human beings need to be."

While I was pondering this subject, an interesting thing happened. One morning as I was putting on my watch I thought about the special bracelets that are worn by the "wanderers" in nursing homes. All the exit doors must be equipped with alarms. Anyone wearing one of these bracelets who exits an alarmed door sets off a very loud signal to alert workers at the facility. It is, of course, for the wanderers' protection, since their minds have lost the right judgment necessary to keep themselves safe.

For some reason, looking at my watch that morning, I wondered if I was putting it on for my protection. Would I get lost if I didn't have it? Would some harm come to me? Have I lost the right judgment necessary to know what is good for me? Drifting into a little sci-fi thinking, I began to wonder who was doing the watching, me or the watch. Finally, I was reminded of a quote from the article mentioned earlier. "Now in the Western world there's this idea that time is more valuable than you are."

**Who cares!!!** Since time is money in our society, a lot of people care. Unfortunately, the logical conclusion is that since time is more valuable than you are and time is money, money must also be more valuable than you are.

Our obsession with time and money is robbing us of our peace of mind. Evan T. Pritchard authored a book entitled *No Word for Time* about how the Native American Algonquin people deal with time. He writes,

> This is a really important issue: A clock is never in the present moment. It's never still. It has this wonderful onward flow, in a sense, but to be in the moment means stepping out of that, getting into a different flow, and experiencing stillness.... The doorway to anything sacred is right under your feet. You're standing on that sacred spot — that portal — but most of the time you're not still. And when you are in motion in your mind and body, just a little bit, then you lose it. Stillness brings you into the sacred, because it brings you into the eternal now.... The root of many ailments seems to be in the mind. Modern research has confirmed that both body and mind heal best when in deep relaxation. They balance themselves out naturally. *That's why stillness is so important. It heals your whole life.*

**Who cares!!!** "Come to me, all you who are weary and find life burdensome, and I will refresh you. Take my yoke upon your shoulders and learn from me, for I am gentle and humble of heart. Your souls will find rest. For my yoke is easy and my burden light."

"Why are you rushing so much?" asked the Rabbi. "I am rushing after my livelihood." the man answered. "And how do you know," said the Rabbi, "that your livelihood is running before you, so you have to rush after it? Perhaps it's behind you, and all you need do is *stand still.*"

# Built Upside Down

Did you hear about the boy who was built upside down, his feet smelled and his nose ran? If you need any evidence that I'm not an intellectual, this one-line story should convince you.

There are times when I feel that I must be built upside down. I say this because I have found that I can live quite happily without the things our present society holds as important. I say this because what is considered exciting in contemporary culture does nothing for me. That is particularly true of our seeming need for action-packed adventure.

A most interesting book was brought to my attention recently, *Waking Up in Time* by Peter Russell. The author says, "If we are to navigate safely through this critical moment of history...it will mean awakening to the wisdom that lies within us all, of which the great sages have always spoken. This is our next step in evolution — not an outer step, but an inner step." He also writes, "There is nothing we have to do or achieve to find inner peace, joy and fulfillment. All that is needed is to remove the *layers of thought* that have kept it hidden." Finally, he asks, "Will we wake up in time and avoid catastrophe? That is still an open question." The interesting thing about this book is that its author is not a wild-eyed fanatic but owns an honors degree in theoretical physics and psychology and a master's degree in computer science.

I write this reflection shortly after the 50th anniversary of the death of a great, though little-known, sage, Peter Maurin, cofounder with Dorothy Day of the Catholic Worker movement. Peter sought to "foster a society based on creed instead of greed, on systematic unselfishness instead of systematic selfishness, of gentle personalism instead of rugged individualism." Our money boldly proclaims, "In God we trust," but our whole economic system gives very little evidence that there's much of that going on. As for systematic selfishness, Calvin, of *Calvin and Hobbes* fame, is walking along and spies something in the grass. "Look!

A quarter!! Wow! I'm rich beyond my dreams! I can have anything I want! All my prayers have been answered!" He then stops and thinks, "Maybe there's more." We then see him on his knees searching in the grass. Greed fosters selfishness. If there's more, we have to have it; we deserve it. If there is more, there are also other people seeking the "more," and gentle personalism gives way to rugged individualism.

Peter Maurin put it this way,

> The world would be better off if people tried to become better. And people would become better if they stopped trying to become better off.... Everybody would be rich if nobody tried to become richer. And nobody would be poor if everybody tried to be the poorest.

Is it any wonder that he is a little-known sage of the past, for who could take seriously such upside-down thinking?

In the meantime, the "layers of thought" we need to remove to find inner peace, joy and fulfillment may be very thick and may require some major digging. The first step, of course, is accepting the fact that they are there, accepting the fact that maybe, just maybe, the way things are is not the way they were meant to be. Peter Maurin sought to build a society "where it is easier for people to be good." Peter Russell, some 50 years later, wonders if we will *wake up in time to* build such a society.

# Land Before Time

Presently I am living in a "mean" time. I am wanting something to happen as soon as possible, and the possible is mostly in the hands of others.

So what am I supposed to do in this meantime? I've been thinking a lot about time, how it plays such an important role in our lives, how we have become its slave. My grandson has a video in the series *Land Before Time*. The film, which I have viewed several times, doesn't do much for me, but the idea does. I think it would have been kind of interesting living before the invention of the clock and the calendar. Lots of people lived then and somehow survived not knowing what time it was. I've always been fascinated by Satchel Paige's question, "How old would you be if you didn't know how old you are?" He had no birth certificate to verify his age.

Our language is filled with references to time. We can't really save time, or waste time, or take time, or set aside time. The only control we have over time is the attitude we have toward it.

Harry Palmer, in an article entitled "Stress, Attitude & Concentration" makes this observation:

> Have you ever noticed that some people have a lot of time and other people don't seem to have any time at all? That's weird. I mean, there are 60 minutes in an hour and 24 hours a day for everyone. But some people spend the 24 hours happy and relaxed, and some people spend the 24 hours serious and stressed. Relaxation and stress determine the consideration of how much time you have. Really we are talking about *free attention*. If you ask a stressful person to do something, they'll say, "Oh, I can't possibly do that. I don't have time!" Yet from their viewpoint, time seems to pass at an agonizingly slow pace. Another person, more relaxed, might say, "Okay, I'll work that in this afternoon. No problem." Yet from their

viewpoint, time is whipping by. Doesn't this seem contradictory? To the person who sees time as passing slowly, there doesn't seem to be much time, but to the person who loses track of time there seems to be a lot of it. Actually time passes at the same speed for both of them. What is different is their ability to concentrate. Concentration requires *free attention.*

What I have tried to learn from all of this is that when I am experiencing a "mean" time I need to examine where I have my attention focused. In so doing, I usually find my attention is not on what's happening now but on what has happened, or might happen, or that I wish would happen. This makes me tense. I can't relax, and my attitude about my work, and my life in general, ends up in the toilet. It reminds me of how a person can allow a weather forecast for the weekend to ruin a perfectly good Tuesday.

Your attitude is determined by that upon which you have your attention — and you are free to place your attention on whatever you wish. If your attention is constantly on things beyond your control, there is bound to be stress, the "dis" kind. Dis-stress is not conducive to being all that you can be.

As hard as it is to accept, the best thing I can do for that something-I-want-to-happen-as-soon-as-possible-but-is-beyond-my-control is to concentrate on the *now.* To freely give my attention to my work, my family, my attitude — in short, to be happy.

So often I have to return to this saying, "Happiness is like a butterfly. The more you chase it, the more it will elude you. When you turn your attention and concentrate on the task at hand, it will come and gently land on your shoulder."

# Excitement: Where to Find It

I must be getting older, since this particular reflection is a result of my anger over a commercial for a supplement. This product's catchy slogan proclaims that while it can't add years to your life it might help to add life to your years. The concept is beautiful, that in years, quantity is not as important at quality. My argument with them is how they define quality.

In the commercial, one "older" couple is sight-seeing. They seem to be happy with their lot until they come upon another couple of comparable age, rafting the white waters of a river. The looks on the faces of the first couple tell it all. Obviously they are failures. As their years have increased, they have obviously forgotten how to be happy, that is, how to live. We, as viewers, are now in the know and will, of course, never allow this to happen to us. We know which supplement to buy.

What bothers me is a basic premise of this commercial and a lot of other commercials. It's the suggestion that one cannot truly be happy unless one is in pretty much of a constant state of excitement. Excitement is defined by the fast pace of the activity in which one is participating. It is also defined by the level of noise generated.

In this meantime, we seem to be so bored with life that the only way we can really enjoy it is to put ourselves at risk of losing it. If you're into some real excitement, shut off the TV, turn off the radio or stereo, and don't just do something, sit there. Sit there in silence. Talk about scary! You'll have to grapple with the demons intent on keeping you from knowing yourself. The greatest excitement comes when you can sit there in silence and be happy with — even love — the imperfect person you are. The excitement increases as you realize that no matter how dull you may perceive it to be, your life has meaning and is *important* in the overall scheme of things. I firmly believe that this excitement will add more life to your years than white-water rafting.

## 2

Celebrating the
Dailiness of Life

# Unfinished and Imperfect, but Content

The renowned religious writer Huston Smith once declared, "In order to live man must believe in that for which he lives." Reading this reminded me of a quotation I refer to often in my personal life. "Meaning transfigures all, once what you are living for and what you are doing has *meaning* for you, it is irrelevant whether you are happy or unhappy, you're *content*. You're not alone in your spirit. You *belong*" (Laurens vanderPost).

I use this message as a measure in my personal life because the concept of happiness or unhappiness being irrelevant fascinates me. In my lifetime we have come full circle on the subject of happiness. Now it is seen as that elusive goal for which everyone searches. Every product featured in TV commercials ultimately promises, as its end result, happiness. It is everyone's goal and, we are told, everyone's right. Even our Founding Fathers spoke of our right to the "pursuit of happiness." I say "full circle" because when I was young being happy was, at times, looked upon as coming from the evil one. There was a maxim that proclaimed, "If it feels good, it must be bad." This came out of our religious upbringing. If I remember correctly, this started with the very first question in my catechism, "Why did God make us?" The answer, as I remember it, was "To know, love and serve Him in this life and be happy with Him in the next." This put God in the category of those who believe in delayed gratification. There was no mention of being happy in this life; that was reserved for the next. We had work to do in this life. This was a powerful message — so much so that some came to the conclusion that the more suffering you endured in this life the happier you would be in the next. Life was not seen as a whole but as the one we live here and then that other one hereafter.

When we begin to see life as a never-ending series of significant and important events, then the message in Huston Smith's quote makes more sense. We also begin to understand better the elusive butterfly of happiness that we talked about in the first chapter. Happiness is not the goal but the feeling one has at reaching the goal. The goal is *living* a day at a time *with meaning.*

A curve ball our present society throws at us is an emphasis on winning. In order to be happy, we feel we must win. "Losers" don't celebrate, they commiserate. Another curve ball is the emphasis on having. There are certain things we believe we just must have in order to be happy. Unfortunately these *must win* and *must have* attitudes are even carried over into our relationships.

One of the words I highlighted in the above quote was *content.* My dictionary defines this word as "Satisfied; not inclined to complain or desire something more or different than one has." I consider myself satisfied, and I ordinarily don't complain, but I must admit I still have desires. One of those desires is to live in a rustic but comfortable home nestled in a wooded area overlooking the Pacific Ocean. There I could become a really famous writer. The key to my success is that I don't allow such desires to upset my peace of mind. Such desires are weighed against my own limitations — some of which may be self-imposed — and the reality of life around me.

You belong! Why were we made? To be happy in this life and ecstatic in the next. To know, love and serve each other. To be human beings — that is, to be true to our nature. Unfinished and imperfect as we may be, we become more peaceful and find true meaning as we become more fully ourselves.

# Fear: Society's Infection

A story I must share:

Three people were walking through a forest when they came upon a beautiful garden. "What an awesome place this is," said the first one. "I wonder who is responsible for such an incredible looking garden."

"But it's not just the way it looks," said the second excitedly, "there's a special feeling here, a very unique and powerful feeling. I wonder what it is."

The third one grabbed his companions by the arms, stopping them short. In a hushed tone he said, "You know things like this don't just happen. It might be a trap. We'd better be careful."

Shortly they happened upon an old man in white robes sitting near a fountain at the center of the garden. The first one asked, "O Wise One, can you tell us what this marvelous looking garden is?"

The old man replied in a sage and sprightly voice, "Why this is the Garden of Life. Haven't you ever seen the Garden of Life before?"

"But, Wise One, what is that special feeling that's here?" the second one asked.

"Why that's the feeling of life. Haven't you ever felt the feeling of life before?"

Then the third one said, "But tell me, sir, is there any danger here that we should watch out for?"

"Oh, yes," replied the wise man, narrowing his eyes and lowering his voice dramatically.

"I thought so," exclaimed the third man with a start. "I'm outta here." And in the blink of an eye he was gone.

"Well," said the old man, "now that the danger is gone, let's enjoy this beautiful garden together" (*Avatar Journal*).

Wasn't it Franklin Roosevelt who said, "We have nothing to fear but fear itself"? He spoke these words in a time of war, but fear remains a significant part of the lives of most people at all times today. Suspicion, skepticism, pessimism and negativity are all strains of this mental virus called fear that has infected our society. Also, infected people become carriers and can be responsible for passing on this virus to generations of humanity.

I'm going way out on a limb here by asking, "Is the world a dangerous place because there are real dangers or because of our beliefs about the dangers?" Reflect on these words from *A Course in Miracles*: "Peace of mind is purely an internal matter. It must begin with your own thoughts and then extend outward. It is from your *peace of mind* that a peaceful perception of the world arises."

It is an indisputable fact that what we fear grows in proportion to our obsession with it. The more we fear a thing, the bigger it becomes, which in turn increases our fear. Are we willing to believe, as the Book I read on a regular basis says, that "Perfect love casts out fear."

Have you ever pondered how, and how much, your skeptical and suspicious beliefs about the world may be influencing the quality of your experience. How many times do we encounter some difficulty in life and hear ourselves saying, "I knew that was going to happen." In other words, expectation confirmed. As this pattern repeats, it reinforces and increases our level of conviction in the belief that the world is full of danger. Then more and more of our energy and attention go into learning strategies and solutions to deal with or avoid the danger.

So how have your walks in the Garden of Life been lately? Have they been enjoyable, unhurried, filled with that special feeling, or do you see danger lurking behind each tree and on the face of everyone you meet. "If you knew Who walks beside you on the way that you have chosen, fear would be impossible" (*A Course in Miracles*).

# Painful Truth

"There are many answers you have received, but have not yet heard" (*A Course in Miracles*). "Truth is won when we have the courage to feel the pain of knowing it." (I don't remember where that one comes from.)

Let's ponder these two truths for a while. Let's face them without fear or frustration. Let's play with them without any thought of winning or losing, right or wrong. Let's not see them as problems to be solved. In fact, if in our pondering together, you begin to feel agitated or upset, set them aside for a while. Agitation is like static on the radio or interference on TV. It is often the cause of our not hearing what we have received.

In a tape series I recently listened to, the speaker used an illustration I found intriguing. He spoke of how in video games all the possible moves and counter moves are programmed in by the maker of the game. He suggested that you may not wish to play chess with a computer game, especially if it is classified as "Master." In this game every conceivable move has been programmed into the game cartridge. He went on to suggest that this is also the case with our lives. Our Maker has programmed into us every conceivable action or reaction to every situation that we will encounter in our lifetime. They might be classified on a scale from *very helpful* to *very harmful*. The best, ideal or perfect action is part of our makeup, as is the worst possible reaction. This reflection gives a whole new meaning to the expression, "That person really knows how to press my buttons." Ultimately, however, we are in charge of our own keyboard.

If we continue with this illustration, we must come to the conclusion that we already have within us all the answers we will ever need to know. Perhaps what we need to do most is learn how to listen. The next step is to have the courage to face and feel the pain some of the answers may cause us.

In the comic strip *For Better or For Worse* two young men were graduating from college. One of them called Weed says, "Grad's on Friday, how did you do on your research project?" Mike responds, "OK.... I called it 'Man's Inhumanity to Man.' You know, it's amazing. Here we have a planet that could sustain us all. Nobody should have to go hungry. Why can't we work together to eliminate starvation and achieve world peace?!!" Weed's answer is short and very much to the point, "There's no money in it."

The frustration of Mike, "Why can't we work together to eliminate starvation and achieve world peace?" is the frustration of all who know that the answer to these problems has been received, but not yet heard. The answer has been programmed into each and every one of us. It isn't something we need to learn. It is part of our very being. The problem is the static in our world that keeps us from hearing the answer.

Although Weed's answer, "There's no money in it" seems flippant, it may be an attempt at avoiding the full brunt of the pain of knowing it is the truth. Take the money out of the manufacture and distribution of weapons of mass destruction and see how quickly they would begin to be eliminated.

Wasn't there a song in the past entitled, "Love Makes the World Go Round"? Like so many other natural energy sources we have abandoned through the years, love has been replaced by money. This is a truth I would just as soon not have won because of the pain I feel in knowing it.

# A Robin's Tale of Woe

"Are not five sparrows sold for a few pennies? Yet not one of them is neglected by God" (Luke 12: 6). This was the centerpiece of the suit brought against God by the grieving Mother Robin. She contended that God had not fulfilled his promise of non-neglect.

She began by telling the jury how in the spring of 2001 she and her husband had decided to settle in Concordia, Kansas. They built their home in a tree along Olive Street. Although they had to put up with a lot of chilly and rainy days in early spring, they were blessed with two healthy offspring. Everything was going along fine until tragedy struck on July 3, 2001. That day, after being buffeted by strong winds the two previous days, the home built by her husband and her was shook loose from its foundation and fell to the ground. Due to the softness of the grass, the babies survived the fall. One remained near the fallen nest, the other landed about three feet away.

The voice of the young mother was filled with sadness as she recounted this frightful event. Naturally, she sought someone to blame. She recalled for the jury how God's Son, in the midst of a storm at sea, was able to calm the wind. Why, she wondered, could he not have done the same thing for her little family?

She went on to tell of her frantic attempt to protect and feed her babies. Her voice broke as she told of how it was too much. She told how she lost the one closest to the fallen nest. Although she needed to grieve, there wasn't time as she turned her full attention to the baby that survived. At this point it was obvious there were tears in God's eyes.

She told of how frightening it was to be nestled in grass, not quite tall enough to hide her, only three feet from a busy street. She spoke of the harrowing experience called the Fourth of July. The rockets and the bombs bursting in air were too close for comfort. She also worried how the polluted air that night would affect her baby. She recalled shielding her baby's featherless body from the 103-degree sun. She was thankful for the shade provided by the tree from which they had fallen. Then she told of how she had to endure the pouring rain on July 9 in order to protect her little one from drowning.

She wanted to know where God was in all of this. She quoted from another disciple of God's Son on the same subject: "Are not two sparrows sold for next to nothing? Yet not a single sparrow falls to the ground without your Father's consent" (Matthew 10: 30). She wanted to know if this meant that God had given His "consent" to this tragedy?

God's defense was to plead insanity. What was viewed by Mother Robin as neglect was seen by God ultimately as an act of love. And, in our world, that can only be classified as insane thinking. In the midst of tragedy we look for causes, but God already sees the effect. Mother Robin could only see that her little ones had fallen to the ground. God knows we all must go there first before we can be lifted up to a better life.

As is true of all my "live" bird stories, this one ends in mystery. The little one who survived disappeared sometime during the night of July 10. Our search to date has been in vain. We have found no evidence of fowl play and none of the robins we've seen has been willing to talk.

# On Discoloring Our Being

"And they lived happily ever after." You'll have to forgive me, but as I write this reflection I'm a bit moody. I've suddenly become impatient for the "ever after." My ability to deal constructively with reality is taking a beating. And to the person who said, "The irony is that a life with no problems doesn't offer the opportunities we must have if we are to grow," I say BULL! Give me no problems and just watch me grow.

There, I feel better now, having spoken the truth to myself. I've been honest with my feelings. I've felt anger and frustration over the way things are. And I don't feel one bit guilty for having these feelings. In fact, having admitted these feelings to myself has brought me a certain peace.

I saw a cartoon recently that I didn't find particularly amusing, but it was very thought provoking. It simply pictured a man sitting in a chair reading a newspaper. The caption read, "When he heard he lost all his money in the market, his hair turned gray overnight. The next day he discovered there was a computer error, and he was not wiped out, but his hair did not turn dark again." Think about it for awhile. We've probably all heard of persons graying prematurely when under a lot of stress. On the other hand, I've never heard of anyone whose hair turned back to its original color overnight.

This got me to thinking about how worrying can discolor our whole being. The hair in this case was simply an outward manifestation of what was happening on the inside. Personally, I know when I start worrying my immune system becomes "out of order." A common cold virus comes to visit, and it's as though I'm powerless to resist. All my fighters have answered a 911 call and are on alert somewhere else. They stand ready to resist an enemy that may or may not attack at an undetermined time in the near or distant future. They are *preoccupied*. Worry and anxiety can cause all kinds of havoc. They interfere with our ability to deal constructively with reality because the reality we are concerned with isn't "real" yet.

People who worry have all kinds of good reasons for doing so. The best I've heard was expressed by Grandma in the *Pickles* comic strip. She said, "Don't tell me worrying doesn't do any good, I know for a fact that at least 80 percent of the things I worry about never happen." So I guess those of us who don't worry a lot should be thankful for those who do.

Again, as *A Course in Miracles* says, "If you knew Who walks besides you on the way you have chosen, fear would be impossible." What does this say about our knowledge of the One who walks beside us? Our fears would seem to reflect our lack of true knowledge of Who walks beside us, whether we make him part of our lives or simply ignore him.

One of the Symptoms of Inner Peace (from a book of the same title by Saskia Davis) is "An increasing tendency to let things happen rather than make them happen." In other words, there's an increasing tendency to *trust* that nothing is going to happen that you and the One walking beside you can't handle together.

The key words in the phrase, "and they lived happily ever after" are "lived happily." The only place you can do that is in the present. The only person who can accomplish that is you.

There's a saying that goes, "Don't walk in front of me, I may not follow. Don't walk behind me, I may not lead. Walk beside me and just be my friend."

He walks beside you as a Friend, so why are you fearful?

# Celebrating the Dailiness of Our Lives

By now you know me and quotations. This one I found in an advertisement I received inviting me to subscribe to the magazine *Tricycle*, subtitled, *The Buddhist Review*. It's from one of its contributors, Charlotte Joko Beck:

> How do we place our cushions? How do we brush our teeth? How do we sweep the floor or slice a carrot? We think that we are here to deal with more important issues, such as problems with our partners, our jobs, our health, and the like. We don't want to bother with the little things, like how we hold our chopsticks, or where to place our spoons. Yet these acts are the stuff of life, moment to moment. It's not a question of importance, it is a question of paying attention, being aware. Why? Because each moment of life is absolute in itself. That's all there is.

Please don't allow the mention of "cushions" and "chopsticks" to be a distraction. Simply take her words at face value, especially when she says, "It's not a question of importance, it is a question of *paying attention, being aware*." A line from a book of daily meditations entitled *Touchstones* adds, "The dailiness of our lives isn't always dramatic and doesn't usually offer great changes. But we are part of an unfolding process." I like the phrase *dailiness of our lives*. From the very little I've seen of it, this would be quite the opposite of the soap opera *Days of Our Lives*. There, everything that happens is dramatic with a capital "D." Of course, it's not just this program; TV in general tends to portray life as always filled with anything but the "dailiness of our lives."

Let's face it, the stuff of our lives, for the most part, is boring with a capital "B" by television's standards. But does it have to be that way? What if we began to pay attention to our stuff? What if we began to be aware that this stuff is part of an unfolding process? I was reminded of the conclusion of one of the parables told by the Man born in a barn: "Since you were dependable in a small matter, I will put you in charge of larger affairs. Come, share your master's joy." Are we willing to believe our reward will be determined by how dependable we are in small matters?

Philip Slater says, "One of the main reasons wealth makes people unhappy is that it gives them too much control over what they experience. They try to translate their fantasies into reality instead of tasting what reality has to offer." One way we do this is by hiring other people to take care of our small matters so we can concentrate on what we consider the larger affairs. Those who take care of the so-called small matters in our society are considered "less than" those taking care of larger affairs. Reality itself offers us small matters in much greater abundance than larger affairs. I don't believe the reward in the parable was to dismiss the need to be dependable in small matters but simply to call forth from this dependable person a greater awareness of larger affairs. The problem with people whose whole lives revolve around larger affairs is they often feel the need to create more larger affairs to keep themselves fulfilled.

Although I don't consider the writing of this reflection a small matter, about halfway through composing this particular one, a larger affair diverted my attention. My first reaction was to begin to think of what small matters I could set aside to focus on this larger affair. Food was no longer a priority. Although sleepy, I decided to simply increase my caffeine intake. Soon I was thinking of the phrase, "It's not a question of importance, it is a question of paying attention, being aware." I became aware that as I neglected the small matters of eating and sleeping the larger affair kept getting larger. I became aware that as I neglected the small matters I was no longer "in charge" of the larger affair.

Each moment of life is absolute in itself, even if the stuff of life we are experiencing seems meaningless. It's our choice: We can either *hate* or *celebrate* the dailiness of our lives.

# Two Geniuses: Einstein and My Mom

"There are only two ways to live your life. One is as though nothing is a miracle. The other is as if everything is." I know very little about his life, but I think I would have liked the author of that quote, Albert Einstein. His genius led him to view life as if everything is a miracle. So isn't it logical that if we all viewed life in such a way we would all be geniuses?

Unfortunately, maybe tragically, the majority of us view ourselves as being far from geniuses. My mother was a genius, and I'm thankful some of that rubbed off on me. She had no formal education past grade school, but she never stopped learning. She never had much in the way of material wealth, but she was rich with patience and a billionaire when it came to love. She had faith that moved many a mountain in her 90 years here on earth. I'll always remember her telling me that she was too busy to be bored with life, how she could not stay in bed when she woke up in the morning. The reason was her mind was filled with all the things she wanted to do that day. At the time, she was living by herself and needed a walker to navigate. Mom was a person who celebrated the "dailiness of life."

One thing in my life that mirrors hers is my habit of taking time each day to make conscious contact with my source of power. Mom had a homemade book of prayers. She would run across something that she liked or that inspired her, and she would add it to her prayer book. Her reading was a daily ritual. There was a time when, as a young "man of the cloth," I thought of how much I had advanced. I felt that Mom was simply "saying prayers" and that I had learned how to "pray" with my own words. In time, however, I believe this false pride was one of the mountains her faith moved on my behalf.

Now I have my own homemade book of prayers. It is my way, as I'm sure it was hers, of meditating. They stressed meditation in the seminary, but there was a tendency to standardize it, and I never felt I measured up. Now I "read and reflect" with no expectations or preconceived ideas of what I want to accomplish. It works for me. If you feel the need for meditation, to make that conscious contact with your source of power daily, it might work for you too.

One of my sources of inspiration is a book whose title reminds me of Mom's thinking: *Each Day a New Beginning*. The offering from that book dated September 20 stays with me, which leads me to believe that I'm meant to share it. "No outside circumstance will offer us full time and forever the security we all long for. And in a like manner, none will adversely interfere with our well-being, except briefly and on occasion." That one deserves a great deal of reflection. I feel certain Mom often returned to her book of prayers when her well-being was adversely interfered with — "briefly and on occasion" — not to feel sorry for herself or to seek someone to blame but that she might have the strength to hang in there, knowing full well that security, happiness and well-being reside within.

This meditation from *Each Day a New Beginning* also reminds us, "Our response to the external conditions of our lives can be greatly altered by our perceptions of those conditions. And *we have control* of that perception. No experience has to demoralize us." If we automatically perceive every circumstance that may adversely interfere with our well-being as the end of the world, we will be in constant turmoil. All outside circumstances are ruled by time. The gift of security placed within us by our Creator is eternal.

I am thankful to my mother and to Albert Einstein, the two geniuses who taught me that life itself is a miracle.

# Letter to a Friend

Please accept the following gift with my compliments. It is one that cannot be purchased with a Mastercard and therefore is priceless. It was penned nearly 500 years ago and continues to inspire today. It is entitled *Letter to a Friend* and is attributed to Fra Giovanni.

> I salute you. I am your friend and my love for you goes deep. There is nothing I can give you which you have not got. But there is much, very much, that while I cannot give it, you can take. No heaven can come to us unless our hearts find rest in today, *take heaven!* No peace lies in the future which is not hidden in the present little instance, *take peace!* The gloom of the world is but a shadow. Behind it, yet within our reach, is joy, *take joy!* Life is so full of meaning and purpose, so full of beauty...that you will find earth but cloaks your heaven. Courage then to claim it, that is all! And so I greet you...with profound esteem and with prayer that for you, now and forever, the day breaks and shadows flee away.

This "Letter" expresses so forcefully what I am *trying* to accomplish in my own life and the wish I have for all of humankind. It also corresponds with the desire I have in writing this book. It reminded me of another gift I received and passed on to you from the modern day author, Huston Smith, "We all carry within us supreme strength, the fullness of wisdom, unquenchable joy. It is never thwarted and cannot be destroyed. But it is hidden deep, which is what makes life a problem." Add to this gift yet another from *A Course in Miracles*: "There is a place in you where there is perfect peace. There is a place in you where nothing is impossible. There is a place in you where the strength of God abides."

The question is: Do we really want perfect peace? Wouldn't that be boring? There is nothing dramatic about peace. Suffering is what people are interested in hearing about. It's what makes for a good TV show. That's what makes the news. In his book *Field Guide to the Soul*, James Thornton writes,

> Most people hold their suffering close and think it the most important thing about themselves. Why? Suffering gives you a job in life, something to do while you're waiting to die. Suffering is known; a familiar funk, a drama. It is what everyone talks about. It is what people find interesting. It is what they use all their lives to distract themselves from facing, who they really are.... The price of this familiarity is high. You wind up renouncing hope and forgetting you have done so.

In other words, we "cling to the old rugged cross" instead of clinging to the Power who overcame the suffering symbolized by the cross. He came to give us peace, not suffering. *Take peace!* James Thornton continues,

> If you let go of your suffering, you may lose sight of who you think you are. You will have to be prepared to find out things about yourself from which your suffering distracted you. You will lose the intense, turbulent drama you adore. You will need to be ready to find another way to live.

Finally, the author reminds us, "Be careful not to find high-minded reasons to cling to your own suffering. It is from your own *real happiness* that you can best work to alleviate the suffering of others."

Remember, "The gloom of the world is but a shadow. Behind it, yet *within your reach*, is joy. *Take joy!*"

Admittedly, more time will be needed to get this gift fully unwrapped, but I will keep working on it and hope you will also.

# Shadows

"The gloom of the world is but a shadow. Behind it, yet within our reach, is joy, *take joy*! (*Letter to a Friend*).

Let's think about shadows for a moment. One of the thoughts that came to my mind was when I used to drive to work to the little town of Glasco. I left early in the morning just as the sun was peeking over the horizon. I always greeted it with "Good morning, sun, you're looking mighty good!" Although there wasn't a verbal response, I believe the greeting was appreciated. From then on it was fun watching the shadow of my "Peacemobile" as it made its way down the valleys and over the hills of the landscape next to the highway. There were times when I could actually wave to my shadow and receive a wave back. I did this when I was not busy waving to all the persons in the cars I met along the way. Although I enjoyed playing with my shadow, I found the many who waved back to me on the road much more enjoyable.

Shadows can be a source of pleasure or fright. The sun can present you with a canvas upon which you can paint your own menagerie of animals with your hands. On the other hand, shadows can frighten us if we are not sure what is causing them. We can dance with our shadows or try to run from them.

I remember a talk given by a priest about shadows. His point was we can only see our shadows when we have our backs to the sun. The longest and darkest shadows are no longer visible if we turn and face the sun. The shadows do not disappear, but as the sun rises higher in the sky they become less ominous, and they are hardly perceptible as the sun is centered directly above us. It is obvious how we can apply this illustration to our own lives. The sun is our Higher Power (God). As long as He/She remains at the center of our lives, shadows are seen for what they really are. Seeing shadows in this light, are we ready to believe that "The gloom of the world is but a shadow"?

Henri Nouwen wrote, "To wait for moments or places where no pain exists, no separation is felt and where all human restlessness has turned into inner peace is waiting for a dreamworld." As long as we are aware and alive, we can expect to have some discomfort, some fear of loss, some doubt. In other words, there will always be shadows in our lives. The good news, however, is that as long as we see them for what they are we can deal with them accordingly. We may even find that we are able to deal with some of them by asking them to dance.

We return once again to a line from A Course in Miracles, "If you knew Who walks besides you on the way that you have chosen, fear would be impossible." There is nothing said about there being only one chosen way or that if you are not walking that "way" the One walking beside you will abandon you. Shadows are not automatic indicators that somehow you've lost your way. The One walking beside you is the Way. Happiness is our birthright. It is also a decision we have to make. We will not be happy unless we consciously choose to be happy. "*Real* happiness is largely independent of circumstances. *It lies in your relationship to them.* It derives from and resides in a certain positive stance toward all the circumstances you meet. It is what makes you independent" (James Thornton).

I hope this trip through shadowland has been of some benefit to you. It was intended to spark some thought on how we view the difficulties we face in our lives. Like our shadows, we can't run from them, but we can turn our attention to the Sun and accept them for what they are.

# Searching Within

An oil well caught fire, and the company called in the experts to put out the blaze. But so intense was the heat that the firefighters could not get within a thousand feet of the rig. The management, in desperation, called the local volunteer fire department to help in any way they could. Half an hour later a dilapidated fire truck rolled down the road and came to an abrupt stop just fifty feet away from the devouring flames. The men jumped out of the truck, sprayed one another, then went on to put out the fire.

The management, in gratitude, held a ceremony some days later at which the courage of the local firemen was commended and their dedication to duty extolled, and an enormous check was presented to the chief of the fire department. When asked by reporters what he planned to do with the check, the chief replied, "Well, the first thing I'm going to do is take the fire truck to a garage and have the damned brakes fixed."

This story from Anthony deMello's book *Taking Flight* illustrates our tendency to look to experts to solve our problems rather than looking within. It also points to the superhuman acts of strength and courage that take place in crises.

One of my favorite posters has a polar bear cub emerging from a cave and saying, "Help me remember, Lord, that nothing is going to happen today that you and me can't handle together." We all need to remember that because it is not great crises that shape our lives but the humdrum of our everyday existence. We also need to remember the superhuman strength available at times of great crises is also available in the midst of our humdrum. Above all, we need to see this strength as coming from within.

A Book I read on a regular basis tells the story of the prophet Elijah's encounter with God on a mountain. God is not in "a strong, heavy wind," nor in "the earthquake," nor in "the fire." God comes as "a tiny whispering sound." We all know what it takes to hear a whisper. We shouldn't have to call in the experts. We may, however, have to take our foot off the brakes.

## 3

# Children: Greatest Gifts, Truest Challenge

# Grandpa's Dilemma

A few years ago I came to the conclusion that being a grandpa without the benefit of having been a father is akin to going directly to the major leagues without the benefit of spending time in the minors. Or, it's like being drafted by a pro team without the benefit of college experience.

The event that primarily prompted this conclusion was a Saturday with my one and only grandson, who was five years old at the time. On this day we were inseparable for about eight hours.

He had spent the night with us, so my experience started at a relatively early hour. Being a morning person, this, in itself, was not a real problem. The problem was that he upset my morning ritual, including my bordering-on-sacred quiet time. There are things I do in the morning that are important for the day's welfare, and if it's going to be a good day they must be done in a certain order.

Children are unaware of the importance of schedules. What is important for them is *now*. My first thought when he awoke at an unexpectedly early hour was not that this would give us more time for bonding. My thought was around all the things I would not get accomplished. I had "important" things that needed to be done. Besides my personal morning ritual, some home repairs were waiting, and a portion of the lawn needed mowing. Thank God I was able to redefine what was most important.

We shared breakfast together. I let him put the bread in the toaster and determine how much butter to put on each slice. I learned that now he prefers to eat each slice laid flat, whereas the last time we ate together he wanted each folded. I took the time to show him how coffee is made in an automatic drip coffee maker. It's always a treat to have his full attention when I am speaking. He had milk, but on opening the refrigerator he spied a bottle of pop with a small amount in the bottom. A power struggle ensued. Since there was no one around to discipline me, I gave in. Later he told Grandma on me. So much for loyalty.

Right after breakfast I found myself outside without so much as the benefit of a trip to my reading room. I even forgot to take my vitamins. Our first stop was the garden. In early spring I had received a free packet of Sunflower seeds, the giant variety. Cody (my grandson) and Papa (me) planted them together. Now, some of them are already taller than Cody. While there, he insisted we water the garden. He made an offer I couldn't refuse.

In the toolshed next to the garden we found a gold mine of potential activities. Cody found the little shovel he used to help plant the Sunflowers. I deftly thought of a way to protect Mother Earth from random gouging. I had wanted to fill some holes in the yard, and I knew where I could remove some dirt that would do the trick. After some discussion and demonstration as to which tool was best suited for each of us, we set about our task. As new tools were introduced, this discussion was repeated. Cody loves to work, a God-given ethic we sometimes don't develop in our young people today. Instead, organized activities have become a way of life at a very early age. The highlight of the day was when, out of the blue, Cody told me I do good work. What a thrill to be recognized in your own lifetime.

If I had been a father, I may have avoided some of the mistakes I've made as a grandpa. I am thankful though for the patience I've developed through the years. Patience is an ingredient I do not often see in young parents during the development of their children. Our society as a whole seems to be intent on not allowing children to be children. Allowing them to do *that* takes a lot of time, patience and that which children can never receive too much of: love.

Take it from a pro who skipped the minors, "It ain't easy, but the effort is worth it, and the rewards are awesome."

# Quality Time

In the comic strip *Born Loser*, Dad says to his young son, "I've been thinking about our relationship, my boy, and have decided we need to spend more quality time together!" The son responds, "That's great, Pop! When?" Dad replies, "Starting right this minute." He puts his arm around the boy's shoulder and continues, "Let's see what's on TV!"

Just what is quality time? It has to do with attitude and attention rather than minutes and hours. This is one of the many lessons I've learned from my relationship with my grandson. It's also why the *Born Loser* incident struck a chord. There isn't any question as to what my grandson understands as quality time. He demands my full attention, and the agenda of our time together must be mutually agreed upon. This may be interpreted as selfish, but it's not. A relationship is a contract, but it includes much more than the legal sense. It is primarily an emotional contract. When I agree to play with my grandson, I need to accept the word "play" as he understands it. If I enter into a contract with him to play, for it to be quality time, I need to play by his rules.

There are negotiables, but they are not implied; they must be worked out each time. For example, if my part of the contract calls simply for my attention without any "hands on" activity, I am allowed to indulge in my caffeine addiction with cup in hand. In most cases, however, my full participation is expected, which requires my giving up the amenities I usually associate with relaxation. When it comes to some work I think I need to do, that is also negotiable if we can come up with a suitable time in the not too distant future when quality time can be resumed. Just last Sunday in the comic strip *Rose is Rose* this was acted out. Mother is busy at home on the computer. Her son comes in with a picture he has just finished coloring. "Look, Momma!" Mother does not appreciate the interruption. "Please, Pasquale! Can't you see I'm too busy right now to make an intelligent comment about your artwork?" Pasquale simply moves on as Mother watches him leave. She then smacks herself on the head with her hand and takes after him. As they sit on the floor together admiring the artwork, Pasquale says, "It's okay to make an unintelligent comment, Momma." Mother responds, "I'm an expert at those."

What always amazes me is that quality time is not tiring to me. I love this comment by Harry Palmer: "You can restore your ability to relax by learning how to concentrate. Concentration, under the right conditions, actually quiets the mind. It opens time up. It creates a relaxed state and restores a confident attitude." My most relaxing quality time with my grandson is when we are concentrating on being creative. A large box brought home from work can be anything we wish it to be.

All of what I've said about quality time with my grandson can be applied to all of our relationships, and should be. This is especially true of our most intimate relationships if we wish them to remain so. It just so happened that on the very same day as the episode of *Born Loser* that began this reflection, the newlyweds in the comic strip *Pickles* returned from their honeymoon. The bride greets her parents: "Hi, Mom and Dad! We're Back!" Mom responds, "Oh, the honeymoon must be over!" The bride corrects her, "No, it's not. Dan and I promised each other we'd make the honeymoon last forever, didn't we, sweetheart?" Dan agrees, "Yes!" Mom and Dad break into uncontrollable laughter, "That's a good one!" Mom turns to Dad and says, "Newlyweds say the darndest things, don't they?" It may sound like an "unintelligent comment," but quality time may be compared to a honeymoon revisited, when two people concentrate wholly and give their full attention to one another.

# Very Best Grandpa

"The Very Best Grandpa in all the world...is what you are to me." That is the proclamation I received in a birthday card from my grandson. Ordinarily I get a little upset with all the shouting we sometimes hear about how "We're number one, we're number one." Now I know how when you reach that pinnacle, euphoria has a tendency to set in and you can't help yourself.

After basking in the glory for about a month, my inquiring mind began to question what it was that made me the "very best." As often happens, I found the answer in the comics. In this particular episode of *Pickles* Grandma is talking with her grandson, "Did you carry the laundry upstairs for me, Nelson?" He answers, "Uh huh." Grandma continues, "Did you sweep the kitchen floor and empty the trash?" Nelson responds, "Yeah." He continues, "I'm going to help grandpa now for a while." Grandma asks, "Help grandpa? What's he doing?" Nelson answers, "Nothing."

After much deliberation I came to the conclusion that I became the "very best grandpa in all the world" (in the eyes of my grandson) by doing nothing.

My whole relationship with my grandson has brought me to understand how backward we are in our thinking. We have been conditioned to view life from the do/have/be mode. If we *do* a good job, we will *have* the things we want, and then we will *be* happy. This thinking always puts our means to gain happiness outside of ourselves. By contrast, the mode intended by our Creator is be/do/have.

One of the branches of the military service suggests in its recruiting material that if you join they will help you "Be all that you can be." I like the motto, but I have a feeling your freedom to be all that you can be might be limited by their idea of what they want you to be or think you should be.

To be all that you can be you need to discover who you are. A most interesting question is one we often hear addressed to someone we may think is acting out of line. That question is,

"Who do you think you are?" We often insert the words "the hell" between the "who" and the "do" to add emphasis. It is an important question because who we think we are may not be who we really are. If we think we are anything other than the work of God, or if we think we are not wholly lovable and wholly loving, then we have not yet discovered who we are. If we still feel we have to *do* something in order to *be* someone, then we have not yet discovered who we are.

The world has enough "go-getters," people out there intent on making a name for themselves. What the world needs now are more "go-givers," people willing to take time out from their go-getting to give.

So when I say I became the best by doing nothing, I'm simply trying to emphasize that all I did was tap into that unique source each and every one of us has of being the best that we can be. That source was implanted in us by our Creator. When you tap into your *being*, your *doing* comes naturally; you don't have to stop and check how others might react or wonder what they might be thinking. The reward is a tremendous sense of peace. That's what you will *have*.

That is the one thing, above all others, that I want to give my grandson: peace. If I can give him that, then I will feel worthy of the title *very best*.

# Boredom and Pokémon

One of the saddest things I've heard recently is a seven-year-old boy's statement that he was bored. He even projected this boredom into the future. He was sure that what he felt would return tomorrow, the day after that and the day after that. My attempt at convincing him otherwise was mostly futile. The only thing that would satisfy him was to promise him something "exciting" and to begin to plan for its arrival.

This greatly disturbed me for two reasons; first, because it is a common reality among young children today and second because I'm not quite sure there is anything I can do about it. It bothers me when I hear teens and adults say they are bored, but it disturbs me much more when I hear it from children. I don't have a real clear memory of my childhood, but one thing I do remember clearly is having a vivid imagination. I don't remember ever being depressed because I didn't have what others had — and I often didn't. My very first football was a round Quaker Oats box stuffed with paper with the ends taped shut. Toys were not bought; they were "manufactured." Games were not "organized"; they were "played." Scores were not "kept" past the end of the game played that day, because the next day all new teams were chosen. Any backyard became a football field one day and a baseball field the next. Each day was a *new* adventure. I didn't wait to be entertained. I did that well enough on my own.

As I said, I don't have any ready-made answers. All I'm doing here is "thinking out loud." Seeing things as I do today, I must say I feel fortunate that television was not a part of my life in my formative years. My beef with television is that it mostly eliminates the need for imagination and in so doing has a tendency to stifle creativity. Instead of finding ways to entertain ourselves, we turn that role over to the "professionals" on TV. We become passive spectators.

Most furniture in living rooms these days is arranged so as to make the TV the center of attention. We sit with our backs to the real world outside to view a fantasy, a fantasy whose main ingredient is excessive action and excitement. Often the only "living" we do in our living rooms is that which we do vicariously through the characters on TV.

In *Letter to a Friend* Fra Giovanni wrote, "Life is so full of meaning and purpose, so full of beauty...that you will find that earth but cloaks your heaven." The reaction of many people to that statement would be, "What a crock!" But if Fra Giovanni is right, to paraphrase an old song, we are looking for heaven in all the wrong places. Life, *as it is*, is full of meaning, purpose and beauty, not life as we would like it to be. Boredom enters in when we think our life sucks because it isn't as exciting as that portrayed in TV commercials. In the comic strip *For Better or For Worse* there was a recent episode in which a couple of college girls go to visit one of the girl's aunts. The niece has done all kinds of things to make herself look "with it." Her hairstyle, the way she is dressed, her jewelry and where she is wearing it all bother her outspoken, older and wiser aunt. The aunt compared what the girl was doing to "spray painting a beautiful rose."

If you find your life boring, maybe it would be good to start scraping away the paint that's built up over the years.

As to my problem with the seven-year-old, I'm in daily contact with my Higher Power, asking for the wisdom and strength to withstand the mighty forces of Pokémon.

# Making Peace Our Rage

All the publicity and debate around gun control makes me think of a recent conversation with my grandson. One reason, I feel, the two of us have a special bond is that I have not forgotten how to play. As you know, an important part of play is make-believe. Being a pacifist, my make-believe excludes guns and fighting. My grandson's make-believe, born from watching so-called cartoons on TV, includes all sorts of weapons of mass destruction and fighting. So we sometimes have a conflict from the beginning.

Having grown up playing "cops and robbers," it's often difficult for me to find fault with the concept of "good guys and bad guys." But then I think that if ever a change is to take place, it will need to begin in the formative years. Maybe if I can plant some seeds in this young mind, they will be brought to fruition in his later life. So I have often frustrated my grandson in my refusal to take up make-believe arms even for the worthy cause of ridding the world of all bad guys. The recent conversation that made my heart leap for joy pertains to this subject. I don't remember all the details of the game we were to play. I do remember that we were going to have to deal with some bad guys who happened to be upstairs. What made it so different this time was that right from the beginning he informed me I wouldn't have to carry a gun. Instead, he handed me a small note pad and a pen. Although he didn't say it in these exact words, I became his special investigator. I interrogated the suspects and read them their rights. Even if I do say so myself, I turned out to be one hell of a good investigator.

As I thought about this incident later, I was reminded of the parable of the Man born in a barn concerning the sowing of seed. As you may recall, some fell on the beaten path, some fell in shallow soil, some fell among the thorns and some fell on good ground and produced the desired results. The Father continues to sow the word even though the desired results are not always immediately forthcoming. I choose to compare what I am doing with my grandson to the seeds that fell among the thorns. So much of what he sees and hears on TV tends to choke any growth of gentle pacifism that may have taken root. The recent incident I just shared with you has encouraged me to continue to hope. God so loves the world that every spring God sends weeds up through the cracks in our concrete jungle. This is to remind us that new life, new growth, will find a way despite our best efforts to the contrary.

This same grandson had a birthday recently, and one of the presents he received was a new bicycle. Now I realize since I am in the "word" business that I possibly pay more attention to titles given to things than most people do. So I'm probably the only one who has a problem being the owner of a "Peacemobile" and having a grandson riding a bicycle called "Street Rage." As you might expect, my grandson loves it. It has splashy colors and even has a small plastic water bottle attached. I'm sure neither the purchaser nor the recipient noticed the name. Unlike his special investigator grandpa, my grandson didn't stop to analyze its title. He saw it only as a terrific means of transportation and freedom — and was off. I only hope and pray that someday *peace* will be his rage.

# Batman and Robin

"Life is a process of letting go, letting go of conditions we can't control, letting go of people — watching them move out of our lives, letting go of times, places, experiences" (*Each Day a New Beginning*).

The longer I live and the more I become in tune with the rhythms of life, the more I become convinced that life has meaning and that I am playing a major role in it. It took me about fifteen minutes to compose that last sentence. I had to check each word, and every thought expressed, against the reality within me and the reality around me.

The reality around is that Batman and his mother have moved from Gotham City, leaving Robin alone to deal with all the bad guys. And frankly, Robin sometimes wonders how he's going to survive. The reality within me is the sure knowledge that this was the right thing to do and that even superheroes like Robin can have trouble letting go. (For those who may not be aware of it: Batman is my grandson, a constant companion for almost six years, and I, of course, am Robin.)

It had been some time since I had experienced a full-scale move. As I read those words, "Life is a process of letting go," I thought of how in the midst of the move it seemed rather that "Life is a process of accumulating material possessions." Without the help of some very special people the move quite possibly may have done me in — and that's hard for a superhero to admit.

Throughout the move, these words from one of the Psalms were constantly on my mind, "Trust in the Lord, be strong: Let your heart take courage, and hope in the Lord." There were times when I didn't feel I wanted my heart to "take courage." I just wanted it to "take cover" till all of this blew over. I experienced the feeling of that guy in the story hanging from a tree limb on the side of a cliff. He heard the voice from above saying all he need do is let go and God would be at the bottom to catch him. The man asked, "Is there anyone else up there?"

My hope during this time was not always in the Lord but rather in thinking that maybe there might be another way.

The meditation I quoted earlier goes on to say,

> Leaving behind anyone or anyplace we have loved may sadden us, but it also provides us opportunities for growth we hadn't imagined. These experiences push us beyond our former selves to deeper understandings of ourselves and others.... Instead of dreading the ending of a time, the departure of a loved one, we must try to appreciate what we have gained already and know that life is fuller for it.

Brave words that this wounded heart will need to ponder for some time. There is no doubt that my life is fuller for the experience, but why, just when one becomes full, is it necessary to pour out from this fullness? Could it be because, as the saying goes, "Love is like water. If it doesn't flow, it stagnates"?

I made bold to say earlier that I am convinced life has meaning and I am playing a major role in it. I say this because it is my hope that someday everyone may have that feeling. I use the word "major" because, in life, there are no minor roles. We seek our "place in the sun" as if somehow the place where we are is not in the sun, but the Son is there. Our worth is not established by education, by our jobs, by money or material possession, by our talents, our looks, our personality. Our worth is established by God. Nothing we do or think or wish or make is necessary to establish our worth. This is the message I hope Batman will take with him and pass on to others. He will always be a superhero in the eyes of God — and also in Robin's eyes.

# Children Know What Is Really Important

Grown-ups like figures. When you tell them that you have made a new friend, they never ask you any questions about essential matters. They never say to you, "What does his voice sound like? What games does he love best? Does he collect butterflies?" Instead they demand, "How old is he? How many brothers has he? How much does he weigh? How much money does his father make?" Only from these figures do they think they have learned anything about him.

If you were to say to grown-ups: "I saw a beautiful house made of rosy brick with geraniums in the windows and doves on the roof," they would not be able to get any idea of that house at all. You would have to say to them: "I saw a house that cost $80,000.00." Then they would exclaim: "Oh, what a pretty house that is!" They are like that. One must not hold it against them. Children should always show great forbearance toward grown-up people. But certainly, *for us who understand life, figures are a matter of indifference.*

For some reason this quotation from *The Little Prince* reminds me of a local news article I read recently. It noted that when the prisoners from the state penitentiary went out to help the surrounding farmers they were forbidden to talk politics. Friendships were forged by talking about "essential matters" like families, friends, the land and our relationship to it.

I've often wondered what would happen if such a moratorium was in place when the leaders of nations meet to talk about peace. What if both sides took out pictures of their children and grandchildren and shared them with each other? What if they were to see these as the "essential matters"? Maybe the differences they were ready to go to war for would become "a matter of indifference."

As it's said, "Life is an adventure to be lived, not a problem to be solved." It seems that the first half of this saying usually applies to us when we are children, the second half to when we are adults. The change seems to come when figures in our lives cease being a matter of indifference. Is that the time when we also cease understanding what is essential in life?

There is One who lived among us for a while who found the answer to that last question to be "yes." He was quite clear concerning his solution to this problem. "Unless you become as little children, you shall not enter the kingdom of heaven." We are to become childlike, not childish.

One young man who grasped this concept fully was Mr. Blue:

You cannot understand how hard it is for one to be practical who hopes for tenderness behind every face, how hard it is for one to be severe and profound who believes himself to be living a story that is glorious and true. Others can be impersonal, but not one who believes that he is on an eminently personal adventure. Others can be important, but not one who is so small that he wonders why anyone save the infinitely kind God should be good to him. Others can be sensible, but not one who knows in his heart how few things really matter. Others can be sober and restrained, but not one who is mad with the loveliness of life and almost blind with its beauty. So others can live with wise men and important men, while I must always presume on those who are kind enough to forgive and weak enough to understand.

My old friends Antoine de Saint Exupery, author of *The Little Prince*, and Myles Connolly, author of *Mr. Blue*, always lift my spirit. They also speak as eloquently as "little children" do about what is really important.

# Important Things That Are Really Unimportant

It all started with an episode in the comic strip *Baby Blues*. The father of the family comes upon one of the children sitting on the floor leaning against a closed door. The dad asks, "What are you doing?" The child answers, "Waiting for mommy to come out of the bathroom to see what we should do." With confidence in his voice the father says, "'Well, maybe I can help. What's the problem?" The child explains, "Hammie knocked over a plant, then poured his juice in the dirt to make mud, and now he's using it to put handprints on the drapes." The father stands there in obvious contemplation. The last scene shows both father and child sitting on the floor waiting for the bathroom door to open.

When I shared this strip with my wife, I just knew what would happen. It now graces the front of our refrigerator. Many times she has accused me of dealing with difficult grandchild problems as did Hammie's father. Never once has she accepted my perfectly good explanation regarding expertise in the matter at hand. Obviously, the Creator would not have created us male and female if both of us weren't needed. Grandpas are needed when it's time to have fun. Grandmas are needed in times of crises. Sometimes I wonder if she really believes I enjoy sitting on the floor waiting for the bathroom door to open.

Further down the page of comic strips that day *Blondie* caught my attention. Dagwood is watching TV. From the TV we hear, "Well, that's all the news for tonight, folks, and we realize that we still have ten minutes of news time left...but we told you everything that is important; the rest didn't seem to matter much.... Hope you enjoy the music. G'night." Dagwood turns to Blondie and comments, "What a weird day.... Even the important things weren't that important." It caught my attention because Dagwood's comment suggests how strong is our tendency to allow others to determine what is important in our lives. Do we watch the news to find out what things of importance happened that day? Do all the important things happen to other people?

Since I stopped watching the news a couple of years ago, I've come to understand how "even the important things weren't that important." Ten minutes of soothing music in most cases would be of more benefit to mankind. To me the important things are those over which I have some influence. The important things are those that touch me physically and/or emotionally daily. The most important things, of course, are not things at all. Linus' statement always comes to mind, "I love mankind; it's people I can't stand." Until we can "stand people," especially those closest to us, our love of "mankind" will ring pretty hollow. Our love for the suffering people of the world will always remain suspect as long as we neglect to love those with whom we rub shoulders every day.

The same paper that featured the comic strips that day also had a powerful editorial by Stephanie Salter of the *San Francisco Examiner*. She chose as the title of her editorial the first half of this quotation from the Buddha, "In separateness lies the world's greatest misery; in compassion lies the world's greatest strength." She also used this beautiful saying from Francis of Assisi, "While you are proclaiming peace with your lips, be careful to have it in your heart." Anyway, she gave me sufficient food for thought the next time I find myself sitting on the floor waiting for the right door to open.

# Children Learn What They Live

Among the many purposes a refrigerator serves, one of the most important is that of a bulletin board. I'd like to share one of the messages found on the front of ours.

> If a child lives with criticism, he learns to be critical....
> If a child lives with hostility, he learns to fight....
> If a child lives with ridicule, he learns to be shy....
> If a child lives with shame, he learns to feel guilty....
> If a child lives with tolerance, he learns to be patient....
> If a child lives with encouragement, he learns confidence....
> If a child lives with praise, he learns to appreciate....
> If a child lives with fairness, he learns justice....
> If a child lives with security, he learns to have faith....
> If a child lives with approval, he learns to like himself....
> If a child lives with acceptance and friendship,
>     he learns to love the world.

Children receive so many mixed messages today it would be good if the above message was posted on the refrigerator in every home. The mixed messages come when parents, living in the same home, have not decided between themselves what values they wish to pass on, the importance of and what kind of discipline is to be administered. This becomes especially complicated for children of divorce who may have to try to adapt to two households whose value systems are, at times, as different as night and day. Added to this are the messages received from peers and that one-eyed monster, the TV.

These thoughts prompted me to reread the beautiful pictorial book *Please Touch*. On one page there is a picture of a little girl sitting on a step leading to a dilapidated shoe repair shop. She is hunched over, and her face shows concern/fear. Opposite this picture are the powerful words,

> Spirit ebbs away with love's decline. Such a fragile
> thing is this life-love-force in a child, easily blunted,

dulled by poverty, disease, ignorance. How terrible to see the light go out of a child's eyes, to feel defensive stiffness growing in hunched little shoulders, sensing mistrust and calculated distance being woven into the fabric of a fresh new life.

In another place we read, "We do not come to believe in ourselves until someone reveals that deep inside us something is valuable, worth listening to, worthy of our trust, sacred to our touch." To me the most touching message in the book proclaims,

> When a child asks about God, what do we name? Someone "up there"...? An invisible person...? Why not answer with the *experience* of love, wonder, creativity that invites children to discover something in themselves. For whatever opens us to become more human is flesh of the God we can know.... Developing a feel for life is developing a feel for God.

Having recently looked into the possibility of buying a "laptop," I got to thinking, and these were my thoughts: The most important laptop anyone can give a young child is the one that automatically takes shape when we sit down. An added feature to this laptop is that it comes with arms that can enfold the child and help with the experience of security. Believe me, it is much cheaper than an electronic one and comes with a life-giving guarantee.

# Martha and Mary

The title of this reflection comes from a familiar story in the Book I read on a regular basis. When Mary had seated herself at the Lord's feet and simply listened to his words, Martha, who was busy with all the details of hospitality, delivered this blunt question: "Lord, doesn't it seem unfair that my sister just sits here while I do all the work? Tell her to come and help me." The Lord's reply is equally strong, "Martha, Martha, you are so upset over all these details: There is only one thing worth being concerned about. Mary has discovered it — and I won't take it away from her."

Recently, just living, I have been overwhelmed by all the details we attend to that are simply distractions from the one thing we need to be concerned about. It may have started with a recent trip to visit friends who had moved to a new housing development. The layout of the majority of the homes had an attached two-car garage protruding out near the street. Since many of the families had recently moved in, the open garage doors revealed all the things they hadn't found room for in the house. There wasn't even room for the vehicles. We are drowning ourselves in things we are convinced will make us happy.

What was it that Mary discovered, "the only thing worth being concerned about?" For me it's "loving relationships." When the Lord came to Mary's house, she gave him her full attention. Her hospitality consisted of "being present" to the Lord — listening in a childlike way, not presuming to know what he wanted. Tragically, today, we don't have time to listen to one another in such a fashion. We are all too busy with the details of our lives. Wives and husbands both must work to maintain the livelihood our society dictates is "normal." Children long for someone to listen to them as Mary listened, but "There isn't time."

What I hear the Lord saying is that he is not interested in how well we may provide for our children materially. What does interest him is how we provide for our children emotionally and spiritually. Everything else is distracting details.

~ 4 ~

Truly Human Progress

# Putting Humanity Together Right

One evening a talkative little five-year-old girl kept interrupting her father, who was busy working on a report. Not wishing to scold her, the father thought of a way to divert her attention. He saw a map of the world in the newspaper, cut the map into small pieces and mixed the pieces thoroughly. Then, he told the little girl it was a game to see how quickly she could put the world together.

Certain of at least an hour of peace and quiet, he went back to work. Within ten minutes, however, the daughter was back and proudly announced that she had already put the world together. "How did you do it so quickly?" the father asked in amazement. "Oh, it was really easy, daddy," she replied. "I turned all the pieces of the map over, and on the other side I saw a picture of a man. So I just put the man's picture together, and *when the man was put together right the world was right too*."

I was reminded of this little story with a message as I was rereading some documents from a church council that took place over thirty years ago. This council proclaimed: "All that people do to secure justice, more widespread brotherhood and a more humane structure of social relationships has more value than advances in technology. Technological development may provide the raw material for human progress, but of itself it is totally unable to bring it into being." In other words, better communication will take place not with a better phone system but when people work toward understanding each other.

This statement from Vatican II turned me on because I border on technological ignorance. It made me feel good that any work I do to further the cause of justice or to bring about better social relationships between people is of far greater importance than the work being done by the scientists in the Bell Laboratories.

I was also buoyed by the realization that I can work toward human progress without ever leaving my house. I don't have to look for a different job. I don't have to join a particular organization. I don't even have to belong to a church.

This may sound simple, but it's very difficult to live out. It seems everything about our society distracts us from the true purpose of life. Everything has to be "action-packed." We have become addicted to excitement. Simplicity is "out." Excitement is "in."

Our friends Calvin and Hobbes help put this in perspective. In one clip, Calvin explains, "People ask why we tolerate a popular culture that celebrates violence and depravity. Because it's entertaining, that's why. If warped values are the price of a vicarious thrill, so be it: Let business respond to consumer demands." Hobbes responds, "The customer is always right." Calvin, in front of the TV, says, "Shock and titillate me: I've got money."

Building a new house may be exciting, but it's a piece of cake compared to establishing a home where people can really grow in love. We probably need fewer of the former but many more of the latter.

This reflection ends as it began: with the wisdom of a little girl. This one is sitting on the steps of a new cathedral. A man stops to admire the structure. "Do you like it?" the girl asks.

"Yes, very much," the man replies.

"I helped build it," the little girl announces.

"You're so little! How did you help?"

"My father is a bricklayer, and every day he worked on this cathedral I brought him his lunch."

Truly human progress awaits the committed work of us all. Please don't sell yourself — or the rest of us — short.

# Classes on Being Human

Over all I feel I had a well-rounded education. The education I value most is what I received after my "formal" education came to an end. That said, I must retract my statement — or at least drop the past tense. My education still continues today.

There is an advertisement somewhere among my things that pictures a tombstone. The inscription reads, "Here lies the mind of John Doe, who stopped thinking at the age of 32." The advertisement was for some educational material. I kept it because it seemed so right. Mr. Doe may have lived until he was 80 without exercising his mind. Our whole being is like a sponge ready to absorb the creation in which God has placed us to live. It is up to us to make sure it doesn't become dry and brittle, incapable of absorbing the new.

"He that to what he sees, adds observation, and to what he reads, reflection, is on the right road to knowledge" (Caleb Colton). The dynamics of learning include, first, what happens — what we see or hear or read — and, second, what we make of it. So in our observations and reflections we consider what an event means to us. Skipping the observation or the reflection is like skipping class.

As a nursing home administrator, I was required, after receiving my license, to attend 60 hours of continuing education over a two-year period in order to renew that license. Maybe we could impose this regulation on humanity in general. Abraham Heschel said, "Being human is difficult. *Becoming human is a lifelong process.* To be truly human is a gift." We have a tendency to take "being human" as a given, yet the daily news is often filled with stories to the contrary. Another quote, by another Abraham, Maslow: "Self-knowledge and self-improvement are very difficult for most people. It usually needs great courage and *long struggle.*"

The great thing is that the course on "being human" and the course on "self-knowledge" require no special text books and are tuition-free. You are, however, required to attend class and study the subject matter.

One of the reference books I have used through the years is entitled *Notes To Myself* by Hugh Prather. The very title speaks of an invaluable tool for learning. Reflecting is making mental notes to yourself. I find writing them down helpful. A favorite passage from this book is worth repeating.

At first I thought that to "be myself" simply meant to act the way I feel. I would ask myself a question such as, "what do I want to say to this person?" and very often the answer was surprisingly negative. It seemed that when I looked inside, the negative feelings were the ones I noticed first.... But I soon found that behind most negative feelings were deeper more positive feelings — *if I held still long enough to look*. The more I attempted to "be me" the more "me's" I found there were. I now see that "being me" means acknowledging all that I feel at the moment, and then taking responsibility for my actions by consciously choosing which level of feelings I am going to respond to.

"Taking responsibility" — that's what this "being human" business is all about. Animals are programmed by their Creator to act in a certain way from birth. That same Creator put us in charge of programming our own actions. Taking responsibility is being fully aware that we have each been given the "ability" to "respond" and that we are expected to use that ability for the common good of all.

That said, I'm aware that I have a lot of homework to do. I'll see you in class.

# Act and React

Sidney J. Harris tells this story:

> I walked with my friend, a Quaker, to the newsstand
> the other night. He bought a paper, thanking the man
> behind the counter. The man didn't even acknowledge
> it. "An impolite fellow isn't he?" I commented. "Oh,
> he's that way every night," shrugged my friend. "Then
> why do you continue to be so polite to him?" I asked.
> "Why not?" inquired my friend, "Why should I let him
> decide how I'm going to act?"
>
> As I thought about this incident later, it occurred to
> me that the important word was "act." My friend *acts*
> toward people; most of us *react* toward them.

My good mother, the good nuns and the good priests all
taught me as they were taught about God. Rather than the "Keeper
of the Stars," he was the keeper of the rules. As one author put it,
God was like the almighty referee. As long as we were playing by
the rules, his influence was merely benign. If we started breaking
rules, he started throwing flags and threatening us with penalties,
the ultimate being ejection from the game.

Whether intended or not, all of this made my inquiring
mind come to the conclusion that this God was making rules
simply to test us. He was certainly not doing it for our benefit.

It took a good many years to rid myself of this image. I
now believe and know that good rules or laws ensure our
freedom rather than impede it. This should also be applied to
laws passed by our government.

Even the most primitive of tribes eventually come up with
rules so that they can live with one another. People living in any
society bump up against one another, so they must learn how
to deal with this reality in a constructive manner.

In one episode of *Peanuts*, Violet is chasing my hero Charlie
Brown. "I'll get you, Charlie Brown. I'll knock your block off!

I'll..." Charlie stops and says, "Wait a minute! Hold everything! We can't carry on like this. We have no right to act this way. The world is filled with problems, people hurting people, people not understanding other people.... Now if we as children can't solve what are relatively minor problems, how can we expect to...." At that moment Violet pokes Charlie in the nose. As Charlie lay dazed on the ground, Violet explains to her friend. "I had to hit him quick.... He was beginning to make sense."

Now, to try to make sense from what I've been trying to say. We need to stop seeing what we refer to as God's laws as being imposed from the outside when in reality they are prescriptions for our mental, emotional and spiritual health.

When we hear that we are to return good for evil, we are most likely to look upon this as a moral injunction, which it is. But it is also a psychological prescription for our emotional health.

Sidney Harris' friend refused to return an insult for an insult because then he would no longer be in command of his own conduct.

Peace of mind cannot be achieved until we become the masters of our own actions and attitudes. To let another determine whether we shall be rude or gracious, elated or depressed, is to give up control over our own personalities, which is ultimately all we possess. The only true possession is self-possession.

Finally, one of the "Criteria for Emotional Maturity" by William C. Menninger, M.D. suggests the same thing. It says that maturity is measured by "the capacity to relate to other people in a consistent manner with mutual satisfaction and helpfulness."

Unfortunately for Charlie, Violet was not emotionally mature.

# Gaining Wisdom

An interesting article I cut out of a magazine a few years ago provides a good introduction to this reflection on gaining wisdom and the quality of life.

High in the mountains of southern Equador, there sits a small isolated village, Vilcabamba, which many consider sacred. There we find the Western Hemisphere's longest living people. Without the benefits of doctors, central heating, telephones or convenience stores these people live their spartan lives. Through stern physical labor and a close relationship with the land, the Vilcabambans typically live to be 90, 100 and beyond.

Investigators point to many factors which might contribute to their graceful aging: low fat diet, little or no alcohol, clean air, daily rigorous exercise. Yet there is something more elusive than all of these prescriptions for good health. One of the investigators refers to it as "spirit" — a spirit for the mixing of generations, old and young alike, a spirit of respect for all living creatures, a spirit of attention for the wisdom of the elderly, a spirit which views joy and suffering as integral parts of the same human mystery.

How often have we heard that it's our advances in science and medicine that are pushing the average life span higher? In our country, where is the average — somewhere in the 70s?

The story of the Vilcabambans seems to blow a hole in that theory. Their average life span is much higher without the benefits of our great advances in science and medicine.

No conclusions can be drawn without all the facts, so I will not attempt to do so. I will say that working in nursing homes has sometimes made me question the benefits of our advances in medicine that add to the quantity of people's lives but have nothing to offer in the way of quality.

The Vilcabambans seem to have the magic formula that addresses both quantity and quality. It's not likely, however, that many Americans would be willing to follow their prescription for good health and their seemingly backward path toward human progress.

What about their "spirit"? Because of my work with the elderly I was particularly interested in the statement about "...a spirit for the mixing of generations, old and young alike" and "...a spirit of attention for the wisdom of the elderly."

In our society, nursing homes are like museums. People go there to view remembrances of the past. Children are brought to nursing homes to perform for the old people. It's not likely that anyone would bring children there to learn, to attend to the wisdom of the elderly.

If I possess any wisdom, it is not the result of the number of years I spent in school. Nor is it the result of the number of books I've read. Wisdom is more the result of life experience and our reflection on it.

As an example, I remember many years ago experiencing a feeling of freedom when I finally kicked perfectionism out of my life. At that point I began to see that even my failures and multiple mistakes could be helpful to me and perhaps to others.

The key to wisdom is our "reflection" on our life experiences. I do not fear going back and dwelling on my mistakes, my perceived failures, and judging them in the light of my history. Have I learned from them? Am I a better person because of them? I do this now so that when I am older and may have more time on my hands than I would like, I'll not dwell on them in a negative or remorseful way.

Ralph Waldo Emerson put it beautifully, "What lies behind us and what lies before us are tiny matters compared to what lies within us." Taking to heart Emerson's words and the wisdom of the Vilcabambans' way of life can impel us on the way toward truly human progress.

# Everything Will Be All Right?

"We can open ourselves to opportunities today. They abound in our lives. No circumstance we find ourselves in is detrimental to our progress. No relationship with someone at work or at home is superfluous to our development. Teachers are everywhere. And as we become ready for a new lesson, one will appear."

My first reaction to the above was "Give me a break!" Are they trying to say that our environment doesn't matter? Are they trying to say that our families and the company we keep can't have any affect on us?

"No barrier, no difficult person, no tumultuous time is designed to interrupt our progress. *All* experiences are simply to teach us what we have yet to learn" (Both quotes from *Each Day a New Beginning*).

My problem is I keep thinking and/or hoping that my learning days will someday be over. I figure once I've learned it all then "barriers, difficult people and tumultuous times" will all be in the past and I will be able to face the future, or at least the present, with complete confidence.

This is a return to a familiar theme of mine that says you're in for a disappointment if you allow yourself to believe, "Someday everything will be all right."

It's all a matter of what we understand by the term "all right." Our concept of all right is too often determined by someone other than ourselves. It may be dictated by the values set forth by the society in which we find ourselves. It may even be determined by the people working in the advertising industry. All right is such an arbitrary term. All right for whom? For us, of course! If everybody would just shape up, everything would be all right!

All right has everything to do with *attitude*. This quote from Chuck Swindol says it all:

> The longer I live, the more I realize the impact of attitude on life. Attitude, to me, is more important than facts. It is more important than the past, than education,

than money, than circumstances, than failure, than successes, than what other people think or say or do. It is more important than appearance, giftedness or skill. It will make or break a company...a church...a home. The remarkable thing is we have a choice every day regarding the attitude we will embrace for that day. We cannot change our past.... We cannot change the fact that people will act in a certain way. We cannot change the inevitable. The only thing we can do is play on the one string we have, and that is our attitude. I am convinced that life is 10 percent what happens to me and 90 percent how I react to it.

I like his use of the word "embrace" with regard to the attitude we hold. We most often hold on to our attitudes very tightly, for better or for worse, till death do us part. That may be all right if the attitude we have chosen to hold is beneficial to our physical, mental and spiritual well-being.

Finally, all of this reminded me of this poem entitled "Our Choice" — author unknown.

I saw them tearing a building down,
    a gang of men in a busy town.
With a yo heave ho and a lusty yell,
    they swung a beam and the side wall fell.
I asked the foreman, 'Are these men skilled,
    skilled, as the men you would hire to build?'
He laughed and said, 'Oh no, indeed,
    common labor is all I need.
I can easily wreck in a day or two
    what builders have taken years to do.'
So, I asked myself as I went my way,
    which of these roles I've tried to play.
Am I a builder who works with care
    who measures life with the rule of square?
Or am I a wrecker who walks the town
    content with the labor of tearing down?

# Martin and Dorothy

In her editorial entitled "In Separateness Lies the World's Misery," Stephanie Salter cited the words of Martin Luther King Jr. "Returning violence for violence multiplies violence, adding deeper darkness to a night already devoid of stars. Darkness cannot drive out darkness; only light can do that. Hate cannot drive out hate; only love can do that."

Of all my heroes who have attained notoriety, Martin Luther King Jr. tops the list. In 1975 I had the privilege of visiting his grave in Atlanta. I had taken a year's leave to travel and study poverty in America. It was a purely personal venture. I purchased a 1969 VW delivery van which I fixed up so I could live in it part of the time. To me the excursion was more of a pilgrimage to visit the people who had greatly influenced my life. One of those, Dorothy Day, was still alive at that time, living and helping the poor in New York City. The other, of course, was Martin Luther King Jr. He had been gunned down in Memphis seven years earlier. I had the opportunity in 1977 to visit the site of this tragedy and pray for world peace with members of the organization Pax Christi.

Dr. King's grave, at that time, was marked with a simple white slab. A small white picket fence surrounded it, with an eternal flame in front. A man with a Polaroid camera offered to take my picture standing near the grave, for a price. It's the only picture I have of the whole pilgrimage. Although this was a moving moment, I felt Dr. King's presence to a greater degree on the streets and walking across the Edmond Pettis Bridge in Selma, Alabama. Although there have been times when I've questioned the contribution TV has made, I know the live pictures of what happened in that first attempt to march on Montgomery changed the history of our nation.

I spent almost two full days in Selma, staying in a campground just outside the city. One day I walked down the main street, which was occupied mostly by white people busy with their shopping. There was very little interaction, very few smiled or greeted one another. One block over was another street that was obviously where the black residents of Selma shopped. As I toured this street, the atmosphere was completely different. There were smiles and laughter, as it seemed everyone knew one another. In my estimation it had nothing to do with the color of their skin. It had to do with their attitude toward life. Persecution tends to draw people together, enabling them to enjoy each day as a gift. "The ultimate measure of a man is not where he stands in moments of comfort and convenience, but where he stands at times of challenge and controversy" (Martin Luther King Jr.).

From Selma I drove the 50-mile march route to Montgomery. There I visited the church pastored by Martin Luther King Sr. where young Martin grew to manhood.

It was the quotation from Stephanie Salter's editorial that jogged these memories I have shared with you. As I recalled these events from the past, however, I couldn't help asking for Martin's guidance in understanding racial events happening in our world today. He didn't have anything specifically to say about "ethnic cleansing," but one quote offers perhaps the only solution possible for crises like these: "Man must evolve, for all human conflicts now require a method which rejects revenge, aggression and retaliation. The foundation of such a method is love."

We may look with pride to our evolution in many areas. But in the area of how we deal with human conflicts, it seems only the clubs we use on each other have evolved and become progressively more lethal.

Thanks, Martin, for trying to bring us back to the teachings of the Man born in a barn and for keeping us on the path toward truly human progress.

# Don't Do Bad Things

Recently I read a comic strip entitled *Non Sequitur*. It had only one scene and it was titled, "Moses and the first draft." Moses is standing in front of the tablets of stone. Written across them is *Don't Do Bad Things*. His eyes are heavenward as he says to God, "It might leave a little too much room for rationalization. Maybe you should try breaking it down to a few specifics...."

My thoughts were: Here is another example, albeit humorous, of how we human beings simply refuse to let God be God. We seem intent to never leave well enough alone. God looked upon all that he had created and saw that it was good. We, on the other hand, look upon the very same creation and see the need for all kinds of alterations.

*Don't Do Bad Things*. I would have enjoyed my religion classes as a child much more if that had been the only commandment I had to memorize. The fact that seems to bug us most about God is his simplicity. God's only concern is that we not do bad things. Since he created us, he knows we have within us the ability to know bad from good; he placed it there. Could it be that it's all the specifics that really cause our rationalizations?

*Don't Do Bad Things*. The utter simplicity of it boggles our mind. I can't remember the exact title, but wasn't there a book that proclaimed everything we need to know in life we learned in kindergarten? And wasn't it the Man born in a barn who assured us that unless we become as little children we shall not enter the kingdom of heaven? (It just struck me that there wasn't any kindergarten when I grew up. I knew there was a flaw in my education somewhere.)

In his book *Conversations With God*, Neale Donald Walsh speaks of our backward thinking, how we seem intent on complicating things. We most often work from the *do/have/be* formula. If I *do* a good job, I will *have* enough money to buy the things I want, then I will *be* happy. What I need to *do* is get a good education with a degree, then I will *have* the right job and *be* successful. Think of examples of how this thinking has controlled your life. This formula places the source of our well-being outside ourselves. The author says we need to remember we are human beings, not human doings. We were created to *be,* not to *do* or to *have.* We need to *be* the source of our own happiness. We need to be the source and not expect it to come to us through what we do or what we have. The formula we need to follow is *be/do/have.*

*Don't Do Bad Things.* Whether we are willing to believe it or not, "our attitudes shape our world." Confronting each day with a negative attitude is sure to complicate any experience. A simple misunderstanding can be exaggerated into a grave situation, requiring the energy of many people to handle it. On the other hand, a patient, trusting, loving attitude can turn a grave situation into a positive learning experience for all affected.

*Don't Do Bad Things.* The Man born in a barn, in his farewell address to his disciples, said, "Peace is my farewell to you, my peace is my gift to you; I do not give it to you as the world gives peace. Don't be distressed or fearful." He was trying to tell his disciples and us that we must *be* peace. The peace the world gives is written on paper. True and lasting peace must first of all be written on the heart, yours and mine. Being distressed and fearful are bad things, don't do them. *Be* at peace with yourself; then whatever you *do* will bring peace to those around you, and your world will *have* peace.

# Working for a New Creation

So, instead of loving what you think is peace, love others and love God above all. And, instead of hating the people you think are warmongers, hate the appetite and the disorder in your own soul, which are the causes of war. If you love peace, then hate injustice, hate tyranny, hate greed — but hate these things in yourself, not in another (Edgar Forand).

How does one take an active role in helping make this world a better place in which to live? That seemingly difficult question has a very simple answer. Note well that the word I used was "simple" not "easy." This reflection is the result of my own personal search for an answer to that question. Each of us is unique and so will our answers be.

In a recent issue of "The Catholic Worker" newspaper there is a beautiful article entitled, "Teaching Peace at Home," written by a young couple with a three-year-old son and a nine-month-old daughter. In this couple's words,

> What we have learned through our experience in our parish work and the Catholic Worker is that the challenge of Christian discipleship is that all children, not just our children, all people, and not just our family, merit our concern and compassion. Of course we have a specific, unalterable, and joyous responsibility to care for our own children, but we also have a moral responsibility to work for a new creation.

Since reading this article, my thoughts have centered on the question, "What am I doing to fulfill my moral responsibility to work for a new creation?" Standing at the kitchen window watching the drama of a mother robin and her little ones after strong winds had knocked their nest from a tree across the street brought to mind how helpless we feel, in most cases, when it comes to alleviating the sufferings of others. But that feeling of helplessness must not overwhelm us. Returning to the article on teaching peace,

> The point is that our empathy must have a purpose. It must push us beyond the temptation to close our eyes and hide ourselves and children in an inwardly focused bubble. It must push us beyond the temptation to see only what we want to see, thereby inspiring hasty, uninformed responses that might be prejudicial, reactive or even violent. It must push us beyond the temptation to become overwhelmed with grief to the point of inaction and despair.

If we can't retreat inside ourselves and try to ignore or block out the problems of the world around us — if we can't become self-righteous and angrily denounce those who are obviously responsible for the problems around us and demand they be punished — if we can't even feel sorry for ourselves and have daily pity parties, then what is left to us?

I've said the answer is "simple" but not "easy." What would happen if one day everyone in the world spent as much time putting on the right attitude as they do the right clothes? What if people became as concerned with what's on the inside as they do about their outward appearance? The old saying will always be true, "You can't give what you don't have." I must be at peace with myself before I can be a peaceful influence in the space I occupy. I must truly love myself before my love for others can be genuine. I must speak the truth to myself before I can speak it to others. It's simple but not easy.

The article on teaching peace concludes, "Our children are God's gift to us, and our gift to them is the world we build for them and with them. We'd better get moving!"

# How About a Spiritual Fitness Center?

$107,670.45! I placed an exclamation mark after that number because I am fascinated by numbers that represent large amounts of money. I am fascinated because I haven't, as yet, had an intimate relationship with a large amount of money and can only imagine what it would be like. I know that the reality may not match the fantasy, and even though I am convinced that money can't buy happiness, I keep toying with the idea that maybe I could use it to make a down payment.

In reality, $107,670.45 is not a large amount of money in our business world. One would be hard pressed to go even a week without reading a headline containing the word "millions" or even "billions." The money is out there, it's just that it is so unevenly distributed.

So where did I get the specific amount, $107,670.45, and what is my point? The amount is that which the Cloud County Community College board of trustees authorized for the purchase of equipment for the fitness center that will be part of the new addition being constructed at the college. As to my point, it might sound pretty weird.

This fitness center, I am assuming, will be promoting *physical* fitness. I was just thinking how great it would be if we could spend even a third of that amount of money to equip a fitness center whose purpose would be to promote *spiritual* fitness. It would be a place where students would come to "get in touch" with who they are.

Wouldn't it be great if the students had a place to go on campus where they could really relax, where they could simply be. I just finished reading a beautiful article entitled, "Finding Inner Peace by Not Doing." The spiritual fitness center I envision would help students relax by not doing. They would be given the opportunity to learn relaxation techniques, to meditate, to learn to get in touch with their true feelings, to be comfortable with themselves.

The spiritual fitness center I envision would have a room filled with motivational tapes, both audio and video. These tapes would not motivate them to be more successful but to find a deeper understanding of themselves and how their actions affect others. Other tapes would motivate them to develop a more loving and intimate relationship with the people closest to them. Still others would motivate them to build a society where all the "men who are created equal" work together to maintain that equality in every facet of their lives.

Another room might be called "Choose Your Therapy." There the students would be given an introduction to the ever-expanding variety of therapies available. They could learn how light, color, sound, aroma, music, laughter, etc., etc., etc., can help them get in touch with their spiritual selves.

Hey, I'm not in any way implying that physical fitness is not important. I do feel it's sometimes overblown, and the motivation for being physically fit at times comes from a desire to be better than others. I'm merely emphasizing that we are mind, body and spirit, and all three need attention. The ultimate goal for all of us is happiness, and true happiness comes from attention to all three. I like James Thornton's definition of happiness:

> It is an inner balance and poise, an awareness of our own center of gravity. It is not something that comes and goes, as all feelings do by their very nature. It is, instead, a state of being in touch with yourself and whatever is a happening around you. Of being able to know your own mind and heart, your own needs — no matter how loud the clamor gets. The happiness our culture asks us to strive for is a flimsy thing, a momentary reaction to passing circumstance. If you try to make yourself happy by the methods that the culture suggests, you will doom yourself to dependence on circumstance you can never control.

I warned you it might sound weird. It might also help you become spiritually fit.

# What Is Your Occupation?

What is your occupation? We all have one, regardless of our age. I'm not asking, What is your profession? or What is your job? or What do you do for a living? I want to know what it is that most occupies your mind.

In my case, the reason I most enjoy my job is because it does not require much occupation of my mind. I am a part-time housekeeper at a healthcare center. I do a good job and know that what I am doing is important for the safety, welfare and comfort of the residents I serve. I've been told I do a good job by those in charge, but more important to me is hearing that affirmation from the residents themselves. I usually bring a cheery disposition and greet everyone with a smile, both residents and staff.

I don't wish to imply that being a housekeeper in a nursing home is a piece of cake. Some *could not* and many more *would not* do what housekeepers are required to do. I'm simply saying that what we do, in most cases, comes naturally, which can also be said of many of the messes we clean up. Anyway, aside from the fact that my wages are hardly "livable," I kind of like my job.

So what do I consider my occupation? What is it that most often occupies my mind, both on and off the job? I like to believe it is being a peacemaker. Thoughts of peace, how I can make it part of my life and part of the lives of those with whom I come in contact occupy my mind a great deal. With peacemaking as my primary occupation, being a loving and attentive husband must be an important part of that occupation. Being a father who is there when his children need him must be part of that occupation. Being interested in the welfare of the community in which I live, as well as the nation and the world, must be part of that occupation.

Some may ask, "Has my job become my occupation?" They may run parallel during working hours, but this should not be the case during all waking hours. Your job may he very important, but, of itself, it is not going to make you a better person. It's your occupation that does that.

~ 5 ~

The Comics:
Today's Wisdom Literature

# Macho and Maturity

If you haven't already figured it out, I have an addiction to *Peanuts*, along with other comics and cartoons. Who was it that said, "Laughter is the music of the soul"?

Ziggy, looking at his image in the mirror, says, "Well, ol' buddy, it's you and me against the world." As a second thought he adds, "Personally, I think we're gonna get creamed."

The little troll in the comic strip *Broomhilda* awakens, stretches and says, "I think I'll do something stupid today. I like to make plans I know I can stick to."

Believe it or not, these two episodes came to mind as I was reviewing the "Criteria for Emotional Maturity" by William C. Menninger, M.D. The first of these criteria — there are seven — is "the ability to deal constructively with reality."

Ziggy came to mind because reality hasn't been all that friendly lately. It seems that the weather never does what I want it to. No matter how hard I work, I never seem to get ahead. To top it off, one of my favorite animals, a cat, scratched and bit me, pretty well putting me out of commission for a week. Talk about getting creamed!

All of this suggested to me that emotional maturity is an ongoing process, not a goal that we reach and hold onto for the rest of our lives.

That's why I brought in the troll. None of us is above doing stupid things. This is another reality with which we must deal constructively. I've always remembered this statement from one of my all-time favorite books, *Mr. Blue*: "The successful conversationalist is not the man who doesn't think stupid things, but the man who does not say the stupid thing he thinks."

Of one thing we can be certain, emotional maturity is not a given with growing up or growing old. It does not happen automatically as the physical body grows or as we add more candles to our birthday cake.

Being of the male gender, I don't particularly like this saying, but I know that it is true: "Some little boys never grow up, their toys just get bigger." As a general rule I feel males have much more trouble with this maturity business than do females.

Recently on a *Dateline* broadcast they had a segment on "What's in a Name." They were talking about how important it was for parents to choose the name of their child carefully. I was surprised that Bill made the list (6th) of those names which conjure up a macho image. It almost made me want to change my name since macho is not something I would ever want to be thought of. The macho man as he is portrayed in movies and on TV knows only how to deal destructively with reality, through violence.

In this vein I am sorry to see that we seem intent on prolonging the myth that survival of the fittest means survival of the biggest and strongest. It is a myth because nature has proven that "there are thousands of little and soft things still abundant in the world that have outlived the fearsome ravenous monsters of ages past" (*The Holy Earth* by Liberty Hyde Bailey).

What we need now are not more macho men but more *gentle*men who will deal constructively with the reality of this world of ours.

# A Good Coach

This incident illustrates why I so love Charlie Brown. Linus comes running out of the house to announce, "Charlie Brown, I just saw the most unbelievable football game ever played...What a comeback! The home team was behind six-to-nothing with only three seconds to play...they had the ball on their own one-yard line." He goes on to tell how they won and ends, "...the fans and players were so happy they were rolling on the ground and hugging each other and dancing and everything! It was fantastic!" Charlie Brown replies, "How did the other team feel?"

Using our imagination, let's listen in on an interview by a TV announcer with the losing coach.

TV Interviewer: You must truly be disappointed. Victory seemed assured and then was snatched from you in the last seconds. Would you care to share your feelings with our millions of viewers?

Coach: First of all, I wish to thank Our Lord Jesus Christ for allowing us to lose. Obviously, today God was not on our side. We will have to do a lot of soul-searching, but I feel right now we were getting pretty proud after winning all those games. This was God's way of knocking us off our high horse. This being our last game, we will have the whole off-season to determine how to get God back on our side.

This particular reflection was inspired after watching some of the Olympic trials and the trophy presentation to the winner of the U.S. Open golf tournament. Most of the winning athletes mentioned God at least once, and the winning golfer mentioned three times how God had been on his side.

I am not here to question the sincerity of these athletes. It probably took some courage to say what they said, and I know the golfer had to overcome a painful injury.

I am here, however, to question the image of a God who has nothing better to do than to determine who is worthy to win a particular race or golf tournament. And I am particularly interested in questioning a God who *takes sides*.

As I was pondering this, I thought of an incident that happened way back when I was in grade school. Maybe it was this incident that helped me set aside the futility of seeing God as taking sides. I was then attending St. Ann's Grade School in Clyde, Kansas. We were invited to participate in a basketball tournament at the public school. St. Ann's had no gym. We practiced on dirt and, to say the least, we lacked knowledge of many aspects of the game itself. You have probably already guessed the outcome of the contest, but the score might surprise you. We lost 105 to 8.

Obviously, God wasn't on our side that day. But how could he not have been — we were all good Catholic boys, taught by the good Sisters of St. Joseph; we even went to church on weekdays.

What I most remember was the reaction of our coach, who happens to be the present chaplain at the Nazareth Motherhouse of the Sisters of St. Joseph. I think I remember a hug, I know there was a pat on the back, assuring us he was proud of us. He helped us realize that we were not losers simply because we lost a game. Since that time I have also come to realize that winning doesn't automatically make a person a winner.

I hope I don't embarrass my coach who has continued to inspire me through the years. But I would like to say his actions back then illustrate the image of God I would like portrayed on TV. Thanks, Coach!

# The Comics and Wisdom

Hobbes questions Calvin, who is sitting under a tree with paper and pencil in hand, "What'ha doin'?" Calvin answers, "Getting rich!" Hobbes responds, "Really?" Calvin explains, "Yep, I'm writing a self-help book: There's a huge market for this stuff." Calvin goes on to explain, "First, you convince people there's something wrong with them. That's easy because advertising has already conditioned people to feel insecure about their weight, looks, social status, sex appeal, and so on. Next you convince them that the problem is not their fault and that they are victims of larger forces. That's easy because that's what people believe anyway. Nobody wants to be responsible for their own situation. Finally, you convince them that with your expert advice and encouragement they can conquer their problem and be happy." Hobbes is impressed, "Ingenious. What problem will you help people solve?" Calvin, "Their addiction to self-help books: My book is called, *Shut Up and Stop Whining: How To Do Something With Your Life Besides Think About Yourself.*" Hobbes interjects, "You should probably wait for the advance before you buy anything." While Calvin regrets, "The problem is...if my program works, I won't be able to write a sequel."

Using comics as a teaching tool and seeing them as a source of inspiration is something that I find real easy to do. I'd go so far as to compare them to the Wisdom Literature found in the Book I read on a regular basis.

This was not always the case. There was a time, I'm sure, when I thought of them as childish. There was a time when I thought of them merely as entertainment. There was a time when I thought of entertainment as anything but educational, let alone inspirational.

That was when my life was compartmentalized. That was when I believed that I could go from the physical to the spiritual world and back at will and know exactly where I was in each of them. That was when I believed that these two worlds were at odds with one another rather than being complimentary. The key was not to let them overlap.

The problem came when I began to become aware that this person I am belongs to both worlds and that goodness and beauty are just as much a part of the physical world as the spiritual.

We used to have a dog named Pepper. Once I was dressed in the morning, my first chore was to take Pepper outside. I will always remember Pepper when I read the verse in the Psalms that proclaims, "I shall awake the dawn." One particular morning the sun was just making its appearance, and it was a glorious sight. I stood for a moment absorbed in and thankful for the event. I wanted to use the word "transfixed," but I thought that might be a bit too much. Anyway, in the midst of this brief moment of ecstasy I felt a tug on the leash. I turned just in time to see Pepper begin to roll around in another dog's recent deposit. The transition from the spiritual to the physical was instantaneous.

True to the saying, "When the student is ready, the teacher appears," I learned a valuable lesson that morning. Pepper taught me that, hey, it's OK to become absorbed for a while in this spiritual stuff, but don't start getting the idea that it's more important than your duty to take care of me.

What did I say? Did I say that the material, the physical, the earthy and mundane are as important as the spiritual? It seems as though I did. What do you think?

# Being the Change We Wish to See

"A human being is a part of the whole, called by us 'universe'.... The delusion (of separation) is a kind of prison for us.... Our task must be to free ourselves from this prison by widening our circle of compassion to embrace all living creatures and the whole of nature in its beauty" (Albert Einstein).

It is interesting to me that one of the greatest minds the world has ever known says, in his own words, the same thing as the Native American elder said to the children in the poem "Lost" (quote on page 146): encouraging them to listen to the trees and the bushes of the forest, which are not lost.

We are lost because we see ourselves as separate, instead of part of the whole. An example came to my mind as I wrote that sentence. In this commercial, we are seated in a car viewing a beautiful waterfall along the side of the road. The sound is what you would expect from a waterfall. As we watch, the side window is rolled up and there is silence. Obviously, we are to be impressed at how well this car keeps out sounds. I see this as a typical illustration of how we try to separate ourselves from the whole.

This quote from Philip Slater illustrates this point: "One of the main reasons wealth makes people unhappy is that it gives them too much control over what they experience. They try to translate their own fantasies into reality instead of tasting what reality has to offer."

It probably won't surprise you when I tell you that all of this reminds me of a *Peanuts* cartoon. In this one Lucy and Linus are looking at the sky at night filled with stars. Lucy declares, "Space is too large, we don't really need all that room. Most of those planets and stars are way too big! The whole solar system needs readjusting." Linus responds, "What can we as individuals do?"

Humanity, thy name is Lucy. We simply seem incapable of leaving well enough alone. We seem incapable of standing still long enough to listen to the rhythm of the universe that has been here much longer than we have. We seem intent on proving that we can improve upon what God has wrought.

It's significant that we refer to Earth as "Mother" because no man would ever work as hard as we expect the Earth to work for us. We never give her a rest to naturally regain her strength and vitality. When she doesn't produce as we think she should, we fill her with chemicals to force her to bear fruit. Could there be any significance that these same chemicals were the major ingredients in the bomb that took the lives of so many people in Oklahoma City?

Here's a wild idea. With all this crazy weather, maybe Nature, who also has the title of "Mother," is rebelling against the way we have been treating her?

Let's end this reflection with a prayer composed by an Objibway Indian:

Sacred One, look at our brokenness.
We know that in all of creation
    only the human family has strayed from the Sacred Way.
We know that we are the ones who are divided
    and we are the ones who must come back together
        to walk in the Sacred Way.
Sacred One, teach us love, compassion and honor
    that we may heal the Earth and heal each other.

Gandhi answers the above question posed by Linus, "We must *be* the change we wish to see in the world."

# Being Comfortable With Questions

In this reflection we will explore the adult mind. Linus is talking with Lucy, "You know what your trouble is? You just don't understand the adult mind...adults are different! You have to be able to read them. I can predict what the average adult will say or do in almost any given situation. This is a must if you are going to survive as a child! Now take Grandma for instance...I can predict exactly what she will say in the following situation. You draw a picture and I'll draw a picture...then you take the two pictures in and show them to Grandma...ask her what picture she thinks is the better. I predict she will look at them and say, 'Why I think they're both very nice.'" The experiment is carried out, and the result is just as Linus predicted. He rather smugly concludes, "You just have to understand the adult mind."

Is Linus' assessment of the adult mind true, and if so what's so wrong with predictability? Is consistency not a good thing?

"Life is an adventure to be lived, not a problem to be solved." When we think of true adventure, predictability or consistency are not part of the equation. It was at least thirty years ago when I heard a workshop speaker utter, "We need to become comfortable with questions and uncomfortable with answers." I remember how the unusualness of this statement struck me, and I couldn't let go of it. After that I would repeat it occasionally to impress my listeners, but I never really grasped its true meaning until it became part of my very being.

We will not be free of all difficulties today or during any period of our lives; there will always be questions. That is predictable! Also predictable is the resistance most people will have to believing this — we want answers. To be comfortable with the questions we must know we are sharing this life, every moment of it, with a Power greater than ourselves. We need not worry about any circumstance. Always we are watched over. As we grow stronger emotionally and spiritually, we learn that all difficulties are truly opportunities for exceptional growth, particularly in our awareness of the truth of existence. All experiences can be taken in stride if we trust that a blessing is intended within each one.

When we try to hold on to predictability or consistency, we tend to stop asking what is the meaning or the message in what is happening. All we see is that circumstances are not to our liking. Those around us are not doing what they are supposed to for our happiness. We see our own experience as the center of events. We forget that our lives are only today's expression in a line of generations before us.

This may seem heavy, because we often have very narrow and limited ways of understanding what happens to us. In this state we become too self-satisfied with our ways of understanding the world. It may be comforting to *think* we understand what's going on. When we let go of that comfort and open ourselves to a more profound awareness, we enter the spiritual realm. Here we learn that *facts are not enough to achieve truth*. We begin to understand that love — in the form of connections with all of creation — is where we find the most profound meaning.

Like Linus, we must learn to survive as children of God. We do this not by reading other people's minds, but our own. We need to learn the skills necessary to meet all of life's challenges. One of the first and most important is the awareness that *we are not in charge*. Rather, *we are being taken care of*. I remember one morning looking east out the kitchen window just as the sun made its appearance. I was not looking forward to that day. Looking at all the "facts" I had to deal with depressed me. Then the picture I saw through the window reminded me that "facts are not enough to achieve truth." The truth is that the God who created that ball of fire I saw that day is looking out for me every moment of every day. That's the only truth I really need to know.

# Growing Heedless and Arrogant

A taste of *Pickles*. In this episode Grandpa is giving some advice to his daughter: "Sylvia, maybe you should try being a little less critical of Dan…You know what they say…before you criticize someone, you should walk a mile in their shoes…That way, when you do criticize them, you're a mile away…and you have their shoes." What better way than with humor to introduce the subject of wisdom?

Each year, in the second week of the Advent season, I read these words from the Man born in a barn: "Yet time will prove where wisdom lies." This year they took on a special significance as I had just been treated to a beautiful article in *Aging Today* by Theodore Roszak, entitled, "In Defense of Wisdom: What Elders Are Empowered To Do."

The theme of the article can be summed up in these short paragraphs:

> Wisdom is — at least potentially — the most common and plentiful resource in the world. It is not in short supply. Why then do we think it is so rare? Because there are forces that make wisdom unwelcome.
>
> They shame it into silence and so neutralize the role it has to play. In an industrial world dominated by scientific precision and technological know-how, by specialists and technicians, by experts in every walk of life, wisdom is crowded out. It does not seem to know the right words, the formulas, the facts. It is not up with the latest.

That phrase, "not up with the latest" describes me perfectly, and I am perfectly content right where I am. So it was with great delight that I read further in this article:

> In the contemporary world, the discussion of wisdom runs into a special barrier. *It is among the powers of the mind that cannot be imitated by a computer.* There are no

programs for making wise choices. Ours is called the information age, but wisdom has little to do with information. After all, the people who are most widely credited with possessing wisdom — Confucius, Jesus, the Buddha — predated the Internet…. The simple fact that our culture was created by people working with little more than their naked wits has become a heresy in our time.

Just one more quote from this article:

The trouble with wisdom is that we have, in a sense, become too smart for our own good in the modern world — smart in ways that seem to have no need for self-examination. In the absence of self-examination, we lose touch with our true motivation and become rigid about values. We quite literally do not know what we are doing. And *we grow heedless and arrogant.*

For Christians, Christmas should be the Great Feast of Self-Examination. Wisdom comes to us not in the form of a professional with a title, but "wrapped in swaddling clothes." It was the *Wise* Men who recognized this fact. Wisdom came into a world of conflict not with military arms. The Prince of Peace came with the arms of an infant, helpless, depending on those around him to recognize that violence, in any form, against any part of his creation, has no place in the kingdom he came to establish.

Time has proven for centuries where wisdom lies, but we, for the most part, continue to be *heedless and arrogant.* How do our values today match up with the values embodied in the life of the One to whom the Wise Men came to give homage? It was G.K. Chesterton who said, "The Christian ideal has not been tried and found wanting. It has been found difficult and left untried."

# Love Is a Many Splintered Thing

Charlie Brown shares a truth he has learned: "My dad likes to have me come down to the barber shop and wait for him...No matter how busy he is, even if the shop is full of customers, he always stops to say 'Hi' to me...I sit here on the bench until six o'clock when he's through, and then we ride home together...It really doesn't take much to make a dad happy."

This reflection is a return to a favorite theme of mine: simplicity. It really, really doesn't take much to make God happy. God does like to have us "show up" and wait for him. God will never be too busy to attend to our needs, and he will be with us on the ride home.

Why do we insist on complicating things in the name of efficiency? We compartmentalize, we specialize, we miss the real point of wholeness. The one and only purpose of our existence is to love one another. I was reminded of this in rereading a letter I received from John, his first one. He is very clear on this matter, "Let us love one another because love is of God; anyone who loves is begotten of God and has knowledge of God. The one without love has known nothing of God for God is love." Is any of this hard to understand? "God is love, and the one who abides in love abides in God and God in him/her."

As one continues to read John's letter, the message remains simple, but its practical application becomes more difficult. "'Whoever loves God must *also* love his brother.... If anyone says, 'My love is fixed on God,' yet hates his brother, he is a liar.... Love has no room for fear; rather, perfect love casts out all fear.... Love is not yet perfect in one who is afraid."

There is one statement in this same letter that always gives me pause, "One who has no love for the brother he/she has seen cannot love the God he/she has not seen." My reaction is to challenge. For me it's much easier to love a God "out there" who is love than to love the people around me I can see and touch and who, frankly, sometimes bug the hell out of me. That's why I've always liked Linus' creed: "I love mankind; it's people I can't stand."

In this light, if ever I get around to writing my autobiography, I already have a title. It comes from Lisa Douglas in an episode of the ancient sitcom "Green Acres." She proclaimed, "Love is a many splintered thing." Those who remember this ancient sitcom will also remember the song title that inspired this mispronunciation, "Love Is a Many Splendored Thing." Is love a source of splendor or splinters? Those who have experienced the real thing know that it's not a question of either/or but of both/and. Whether I want it to be so or not, the test of my love for God is in my love for those closest to me, and that is scary.

A recent quotation reminded me of what all of this has to do with our health. The quotation is from John Robbins, "It has been liberating to see that health comes from learning to live in vibrant harmony with ourselves, with the natural world, and with one another." The history of the human race is littered with stories of plagues that wiped out a part of a population. I wonder if all the figures were compared, would it not be true that the greatest number of deaths have been caused by the plague of hate.

The only vaccination we have against the onslaught of this plague in our society today is to learn "to live in vibrant harmony with ourselves, the natural world, and one another." I believe "vibrant" here means more than peaceful coexistence and that we need, as John says, to "love in deed and in truth and not merely talk about it."

# Stinking Thinking

My thoughts in this reflection may be grouped under the heading, "The Measure of a Man/Woman." These thoughts are particularly appropriate at the end of a school year. Graduation, grade cards, diplomas, congratulations, gifts, recognition, sweet sorrow, the promise of a bright future.

How do we measure a person? What criteria do we use? In an episode of *For Better or For Worse* two young men who have decided to enter the field of photography after graduation are talking. One complains to the other, "My Dad still wants me to go into his business, Mike. I told him I was serious about being a photographer. He said photography was a hobby and if I was serious I'd take accounting or marketing and work with him. It's the old 'bottom line' again. He says he wants me to have a good living...I just want to have a good life."

How do we measure a person? What criteria do we use? Do we focus on what one does to make a "good living"? Or do we focus on what one does to make a "good life"? Is it possible to have a good life without making a good living? When faced with these questions, I often return to the copy of "The Meaning of Success" by Robert Louis Stevenson I have attached to the front of our refrigerator:

> That man is a success who has lived well, laughed often and loved much; who has gained the respect of intelligent men and the love of children.... who never lacked appreciation of earth's beauty or failed to express it; who looked for the best in others and gave the best he had.

As I read his definition this time, I deliberately decided to leave out two phrases, "...who has filled his niche and accomplished his task; who leaves the world better than he found it whether by a perfect poem or a rescued soul...." I made this decision because that section seemed to buy into our "task-oriented" values.

In order to *be* someone we have to *do* something. We have to make something of ourselves. And what we have to *do* is not even of our own choosing, it is determined by the society in which we live.

This to me is, as they say in A.A., "stinking thinking." We are so programmed to think this way we find it extremely difficult to believe that "Our worth is not established by teaching or learning. Our worth is established by God. Nothing we do or think or wish or make is necessary to establish our worth.... We are the work of God and his work is wholly lovable and wholly loving. This is how we must think of ourselves in our hearts because that is what we are" (*A Course in Miracles*).

How do we measure a person? What criteria do we use? I spoke in the beginning of graduations, grade cards and diplomas. So much of the criteria we use are centered on competition. How was a person measured before schools, I.Q. tests, the S.A.T.? How about before there were organized athletic events, talent shows, beauty contests, quiz shows, academic bowls, etc., etc., etc. We may truly believe in our hearts that none of these institutions or events can measure a person, but our society continues to label us winners or losers based on what is seen on the surface.

My favorite quotation concerning education comes from J. Krishnamurti:

> Without an integrated understanding of life, our individual and collective problems will only deepen and extend. The purpose of education is not to produce mere scholars, technicians and job hunters, but integrated men and women who are *free from fear*; for only between such human beings can there be *enduring peace*.

How do we measure a person? What criteria do we use? Each of us as individuals must ask ourselves these questions, for we are the society in which we live. Could it be our answers will be determined by how free we are of fear?

# Gender Differences

A lot has been written about gender differences since we found out men are from Mars and women from Venus. I found a very humorous example of these differences in my favorite source of inspiration, the comics.

In the comic strip *Pickles*, Sylvia and Dan are newlyweds. In a three-part episode we witnessed this exchange. Dan: "Is something wrong, Sylvia? You look like you're in deep thought." Sylvia: "Dan, I'm about to make a life-altering, gut-wrenching, earth-shattering decision." Dan: "It's me, isn't it? You're sorry you married me, aren't you? Well, don't be hasty — I can change. I can help more with the cooking. I'll do the laundry, I'll...." Sylvia interrupts, "No, Dan. That isn't it at all. But keep talking, Dear, I like where this is going."

The next day: Dan: "So what is this big mysterious decision you have to make, Sylvia? Oh! I'll bet I know what it is, it's about having a baby, isn't it? Wait a minute...you're not...you know...with child...right now, are you?" Sylvia: "No, not unless we count you."

The third day: You can almost hear the frustration in Dan's voice, "Okay, so you have this monumental decision to make. It's not about our marriage, or about having a baby. It must be your career, you want to switch jobs or something?" Sylvia: "No, I told you this was a *big* decision." Dan: "Well, now you're scaring me. Tell me, what *is* it?" Sylvia: "I'm thinking very seriously about getting my hair cut."

Dan will have learned some very important lessons in life if he takes to heart what he has just experienced. He will have learned that he is not the center of his wife's universe at all times. This is sometimes a tough one for the male ego to swallow. He will have learned that jumping to conclusions with regard to what his wife is thinking is very risky. He will have learned that following the male instinct to jump right in there and "fix it" isn't always the best way to deal with every situation. It is hoped, however, that the greatest lesson he will have learned is to accept that major decisions on the part of another still remain "major" regardless of our assessment of them. In other words, "important" is a very relative term.

All of this reminded me of a statement from *Each Day a New Beginning:* "Nurturing a meaningful relationship with another human being takes patience, even when you don't have any. It takes tolerance, even if we don't feel it. It takes selflessness, at those very moments our own ego is crying for attention." Another important piece to the puzzle is tact. Returning to *Pickles,* Grandma is busy painting a picture. She asks Grandpa, "How do you like my painting?" Grandpa, standing with a friend, is quick to reply, "I love it!" Grandma muses, "Picasso once said, 'Art is a lie that tells the truth.'" As they walk away, Grandpa says to his friend, "I think I know what he means...Whenever Opal asks me if I like her art, I always lie, and that's the truth."

A *sense of humor* is such an important part of any healthy and meaningful relationship. It's right up there with the most important component: communication. A married couple was returning from the funeral of Uncle George, who lived with them for twenty years and had been such a nuisance he had almost succeeded in wrecking their marriage. "There is something I have to say to you, dear," said the man. "If it hadn't been for my love for you, I wouldn't have put up with your Uncle George for a single day." "My Uncle George!" she exclaimed in horror. "I thought he was *your* Uncle George!" (*Taking Flight*).

# Do You Believe in Hell?

Once again we turn to the wisdom contained in the comics. *Over the Hedge* is not one I read regularly. The first time I saw it, I read it as *Over the Edge*, and I must say it is a little of that. In a recent episode the Turtle is asking the Raccoon a series of questions. "Do you believe in Santa Claus...the Easter Bunny...the Tooth Fairy?" The answer in each case is, "Yes!" He then asks, "Do you believe in hell?" After a big sigh the Raccoon answers, "Don't be ridiculous...Why would a loving God create a special place of torment for his creations, when he has a perfectly good torture chamber right here on earth?"

Do you believe in hell? Like so many questions we've asked ourselves, or have been asked, the answer ultimately lies within. In other words, the torture chamber is ultimately of our own making. When we find ourselves in a "hell of a mess," it's ultimately our reaction to the mess that creates the hell.

Hell is not a place so that we must ask, "Where is it?" Hell is an attitude so that we ask, "What is it?" For the sake of argument, let's define hell as one's inability to live at peace with unsolved problems. For so many, the greatest problem is their thinking rather than the situations they have to deal with. Alan Watts said, "At times almost all of us envy the animals. They suffer and die, but do not seem to make a 'problem' of it." Unlike the animals we have a strong tendency to complicate what is very simple. We give this attitude we call hell a dwelling place within us. This hell becomes a hotbed for the growth of such things as self-pity, resentment, anger and false guilt.

In order to get out of this hell, or get the hell out of us, we have to accept a fact of life: life involves much problem solving, and a necessary ingredient for sane living is the ability to *peacefully endure* until a solution is discovered. Another necessary ingredient is letting go of the idea that there is only one possible solution. We get the hell out by not tying up all of our energies in the unpleasantness and hopelessness of a problem we may be facing.

# The Man Born in a Barn

# Born in a Barn

"What's the matter, were you born in a barn?" That question, which I never hear much any more, was always directed at someone who came into the house and left the door open.

In thinking about that question recently, I was reminded of the fact that there is one very famous person in history who would be able to answer "Yes." Then I began to think of all the doors he left open. In fact, I don't believe he left any doors closed. One might say it was his habit of opening doors and not closing them that eventually caused his death. It seems appropriate that this death took place out of doors.

Perhaps we don't hear that question much these days because, through the years, we have invented ways to make sure that doors automatically close.

This is true physically, but unfortunately it is true, even on a grander scale, mentally. Our minds and hearts, it seems, possess automatic door-closers, and they are often activated by the environment in which we find ourselves.

The rich and even the shrinking middle class automatically close the door of their minds when it comes to dealing with the ever-increasing poor population. They often think that the poor are lazy, that if they really wanted to they could make something of themselves. The Man born in a barn had a special love and concern for the poor.

Many who are white automatically close their minds concerning people of color and consider them inferior (except maybe in sports). Add "Christian" to white, and you have one of the best automatic closures invented. Wouldn't it be great if all the unenlightened were suddenly converted? There are so many in that class: Muslims, Buddhists, Jews, etc., etc. Then there are those who seem to be happy with no religious affiliation — of course, we know they can't really be happy.

Those who are normal automatically close their minds toward those who are gay. That sentence was a little test. If you were comfortable with my use of the word "normal," then you most likely see gays as abnormal and may feel sorry for them. However, many see them simply as sinners who only need repent and all will be well. I just can't see the Man born in a barn perceiving them in either of these ways.

Titles have always been great door-closers, and once they are in place they act as dead bolts. We have Conservatives vs. Liberals, Republicans vs. Democrats, Right-to-Life vs. Pro-Choice, etc., etc.

All of this reminds me of the question Calvin once asked of Hobbes, "Do you believe in the devil? You know, a supreme evil being dedicated to the temptation, corruption and destruction of man?" Hobbes responds, "I'm not sure man needs the help."

Finally, an ancient rabbi once asked his pupils how they could tell when the night had ended and the day was on its way back. "Could it be," asked one student, "when you see an animal in the distance and can tell whether it is a sheep or a dog?" "No," answered the Rabbi.

"Could it be," asked another, "when you can look at a tree in the distance and can tell whether it is a fig tree or a peach tree?" "No," answered the Rabbi. "It is when you can look on the face of any woman or man and see that she or he is your sister or brother. Because if you cannot do this, then no matter what time it is, it is still night."

The Man born in a barn was born to open the doors to dawn.

# Defining and Finding One's Self

Reviewing the reflections in this book, I wondered if I should begin to refer to myself as an anthologist rather than a writer. As you may have noticed, sometimes as much as half of a reflection is made up of quotes from other sources.

The reasoning behind using so many quotes comes from an old monastery rule: "Do not speak unless you can improve on the silence." When I use a quote, it's usually because I have determined I cannot improve on what has been said, and I want to be sure you have a chance to hear it also.

There is this story of a man who was lost in the woods. As he was searching for the right direction, he saw another man approaching. He almost wept with joy, assured that he was rescued. Unfortunately the other man was also lost. Together, however, they were able to determine which ways not to go.

We are all on an incredible journey. I use the word "incredible" advisedly. For what lies in store for each of us on the other side of death's door is likely beyond any image our wildest imagination can produce. On this journey we run into all kinds of people. These people, whether they know it or not, are all seeking the same thing. Whenever I hear or see something said by these fellow travelers that has been helpful to me, I want to pass it on. I sometimes feel lost, in need of some encouragement and direction. Strangely enough, when I'm in this mood I am much more comfortable receiving help from one who I know is also sometimes lost. I prefer to quote from people who still have questions. I'm turned off by those who have all the answers.

There is a poignant modern parable about a man who sold a flock of homing pigeons to an ornithologist who lived in a town twenty-five miles away. To ground the pigeons in their new hutch, the ornithologist clipped the wings of the birds so they could not return to their original home. Two weeks later, however, the first owner looked out the window; there, trudging down the road, were the pigeons, coming back to their natal roost. Unable to fly, the birds had walked twenty-five miles, on sore and bloody feet, to the spot that instinct told them was their own true home.

We (so-called) rational animals have a similar homing device. We know in our hearts that our true home exists in that place or state where we can experience true and lasting fulfillment. In that place, faith and hope will no longer be necessary.

In this meantime we also know that we cannot make this trip home alone. If our hearts have not been completely hardened, we know that some of our fellow travelers are, at this moment, starving to death. That should distress us. On the other hand, some of our fellow travelers are, at this moment, living in luxury, about which, whether we want to or not, we sometimes have dreams. That should distress us even more.

There is one person who not only claimed he knew the way but proclaimed himself to *be* the Way. The problem is he was born in a barn. He made bold to say that he didn't even have a place to lay his head, and he died a criminal's death nailed to a cross. What a bummer! On top of all this, he said I have no right to blame others for my problems and that I am to leave all judgments to him. Bummer!!

"We couldn't find ourselves because we hadn't defined ourselves." Nobody asked for this long explanation as to why I use so many quotes. So I guess it was for my benefit — just another attempt to define myself so I can eventually find myself.

# The First Christmas

I've been thinking again about the Vilcabambans (whom I introduced in Chapter 4, page 76), the people of the mountains of southern Equador who live not only a rugged, healthy life but also with spirit, "...a spirit which views joy and suffering as integral parts of the same human mystery."

The word that is most important in that statement is "integral." The dictionary defines integral as "constituting an essential part of a whole necessary for completeness, intrinsic."

The Vilcabambans, whom we would most likely refer to as primitive, have come to the realization that for the human mystery to be complete both joy and suffering are essential parts.

On the other hand, we in the good old U.S. of A., the enlightened ones, try our darndest to prove this fact to be false. Suffering still remains on the top of our list of things we hate the most.

I found an essay by media analyst Jeff Greenfield on one of the evening newscasts to be most interesting. He felt that maybe the media might have some obligation to tone down the emphasis on Christmas being the most joyous of all occasions. He was referring to the feeling that if you cannot find happiness during this season there must be something intrinsically wrong with you.

Christmas, the true story, proves beyond the shadow of a doubt the truth that joy and suffering are integral parts of the same human mystery.

A stable is a stable is a stable — no matter how much deodorizing we may do. Joseph and Mary were human beings with all the emotions each of us possesses. Shepherds were not the type of people to whom you would ordinarily send birth announcements. Personal hygiene was not readily available to them.

We sing sweetly of the Three Kings and their presents, which tends to make us forget it was their presence that prompted a jealous king to murder those we refer to as the Holy Innocents.

The angels sang of peace on earth that first Christmas — did the heavenly scriptwriter make a mistake? It was sung to persons of good will, to persons of justice, of love. It was offered to persons who understand joy and suffering as integral parts of the same human mystery. Peace is not an idea that may suddenly dawn on us. Peace is an attitude of compassion. Compassion means suffering with, not shielding from.

Please don't think I'm suggesting that we need to tone down our Christmas joy, that we need somehow to dwell morbidly on our suffering so that we might find a balance. I'm simply suggesting it is wise not to be overly sad or angry or upset if all your holiday plans don't work out as hoped. Those who experienced the first Christmas will feel very close to you. Do not feel you've failed somehow if your season isn't as idyllic as those spoken of and shown on Christmas cards.

"It is wrong when we look for one lifetime to settle the human heart, quiet its every fear, meet its expectations and end its waiting. There is beauty and meaning in our waiting if we can sort out in our own minds what we are waiting for, whom we await, why we wait" (*A Course in Miracles*).

In this book I have referred to the person whose birth we celebrate at Christmas as the "Man born in a barn." I do this as a reminder of the human origin of the one I've freely chosen to follow. I choose to follow not because he is a king, a prince, an almighty one, but because he not only told me but showed me that joy and suffering are essential parts of my life until my waiting comes to an end.

# Christmas: A Celebration of Our Humanity

*Close Your Eyes When Praying* by Virginia Cary Hudson is a series of Sunday School lessons Hudson taught to a class of young women at a church in Kentucky. While reading it, I found a most delightful Christmas story in this book.

Hudson recalled to the class how she took her four-year-old granddaughter, Beverly, to see Santa Claus at a department store. "I thought it would give her a thrill." It didn't. "Santa asked what she wanted for Christmas, and she informed him in no uncertain words that she was telling only grandmother what she wanted." Later she asked Beverly, "Didn't you like Santa Claus?" Her reply was simply, "No." As to why, Beverly explained, "I don't trust anybody whose whiskers are tied on."

That same night, after her prayers, Beverly asked, "Grandmother, when I get to heaven and sit on God's lap, will you be there?" Without waiting for a reply she continued, "Well if you are not there with me and God has his whiskers tied on, I'll tell you now, I'm leaving."

In the Christmas season one thinks of birth: "A child is born to us, a son is given to us." Yet we also think of rejection. The Man born in a barn "came among his own, and his own received him not." So it's a question of whether we are willing to accept a God who showed enough trust in us to put himself in our hands. Whether we are willing to accept a God who became one of us to proclaim, "See, it's OK to be human!" Whether we are willing to accept the challenge of him who said, "Love one another as I have loved you." There is a saying, "Don't walk in front of me, I may not follow. Don't walk behind me, I may not lead. Walk beside me and just be my friend." Christmas commemorates the day God came to walk beside us and be our friend.

Another of my favorites from Gertrud von LeFort:

Today we can travel with astonishing speed from one country to another.... But the easier and surer our planes lift us to the heavens, the further heaven recedes from our reach. For what threatens to get lost in spite of all the brilliant inventions and technical progress is man himself and his humanity, and that is where the Christmas miracle took place, and that is where it will have to be reenacted again and again. It is not the precision of our instruments that counts but our hearts which must open, our ears which must listen, our hands that must stretch out to others. In short it is our humanity that is being celebrated on this sacred night.

"Merry Christmas!" Linus proclaims on the front of one of my favorite Christmas cards. He continues, "Certainly we should put aside our differences and try to be kind during this season. But why does it have to be for just one time of the year? Why can't kindness prevail through all the seasons?" Lucy greets us as we open the card with, "What are you, some kind of fanatic or something?"

This reminded me of a cartoon that pictured a large crowd in an arena watching Christians being eaten by lions. Two in the crowd are highlighted as one says to the other, "I'm a Christian too, but I'm not fanatical about it.

I strongly feel that until we all become a bit more "fanatical" the sentiment of having "kindness prevail through all the seasons" will remain just a humorous saying on a *Peanuts* Christmas card.

So I guess my wish for myself and for all of you, my readers, is that we all become food worthy of the lions.

# The Best Man

"And the day came when the risk to remain tight in the bud was more painful than the risk it took to bloom" (Anais Nin). This quotation came to me as I was reviewing some of my "muddle," and I thought of another unique experience I had while a pastor in New Almelo, Kansas. During the years I spent there, my church came out of its tight bud and began to bloom in the fields of ecumenism.

Two of the four years I was there I shared the large two-story stone rectory with a young man. He had just returned from serving in Vietnam and had been hired as a teacher in the local grade school. He had taught there before he went into the service, so our church board had no trouble approving his stay in the rectory. Bob was a Methodist. During the week he attended daily Mass. On weekends he went to the Methodist church in his hometown. Bob had come to know who he was, was comfortable with who he was, and made those with whom he came in contact comfortable. His religious affiliation certainly contributed to his comfort, but most of it had to do with the fact that he had developed a special friendship with the Man born in a barn.

In the latter part of the second year, Bob proposed to a young woman he had been courting. She accepted his proposal and they set a date. As the preparations for the wedding began, I wondered how I might be a part of it. I was completely taken by surprise when Bob asked me if I would be his best man. My first reaction was, "Impossible!" The more I thought about it and prayed about it, however, the less impossible it became. My other choices were simply to attend as a guest or stand in the sanctuary with two other ministers and witness the exchange of vows. Bob had an older brother, but at this juncture in his life he felt closer to me. So we agreed I was the "best" man for the job. I cleared my decision with the parishioners, at least half of whom had received invitations to the wedding.

So on the day of the wedding I replaced my Roman collar with a bow tie and did my best to be the best man Bob so deserved. Later, when I showed a picture of the wedding party to friends who had not been present, they all commented on how I displayed the biggest smile in the group. Perhaps at the time the picture was taken I was thinking of how far we had come. It reflected how right I felt in the decision I had made. When we recited together the Lord's Prayer, the kingdom I prayed would come was one of love, not laws, one of inclusion, not exclusion. Bob and his wife recently celebrated their 25th wedding anniversary.

I would like to conclude this reflection by taking the risk of sharing a delightful story from Father Anthony de Mello in his book *Taking Flight*. I use the word "delightful" because in its humor it shines a bright light on what was and on how far we have advanced.

When Sister asked the children in her class what they wanted to be when they grew up, Tommy said he wanted to be a pilot. Elsie wanted to be a doctor. Bobby, to Sister's great joy, said he wanted to be a priest. Then Mary stood up and declared she wanted to be a prostitute. "What was that again, Mary?" Sister asked. "When I grow up," said Mary with an air of someone who knew exactly what she wanted, "I shall be a prostitute." Mary was immediately taken to the parish priest. "Tell me what happened in your own words," the priest said. Mary replied, "Sister asked me what I wanted to become when I grew up, and I said I wanted to become a prostitute." "Did you say *prostitute*?" "Yes," was Mary's reply. "Heavens! What a relief! We all thought you said you were going to become a Protestant"!

# Dealing With God's Contempt

Once there was a woman who had a dream while traveling in India. The dream told her to ask a beggar for a gift. The woman found an old man in the street who reached into his gunnysack at her request and pulled out a diamond bigger than a golf ball. "This is all I have," he said, "so this must be the gift." Sputtering, the woman asked the beggar if he knew what he was doing. "Yes, of course," said the old man. "I found it in the swamp just outside the city." The woman thanked the beggar for his gift and went to the swamp to meditate until dusk. Then she returned to the beggar and handed him the jewel. "Instead of the diamond," she said, "please teach me the wisdom that let you give me this gift."

This story is from an issue of the newsletter *Ministry of Money*. It arrived shortly after I was surprised by the intensity in the language of the Man born in a barn found in the sixteenth Chapter of Luke. It is in answer to the Pharisees deriding him for saying, "You cannot give yourself to God and money." To these avaricious men he addressed these words, "You justify yourselves in the eyes of men, but God reads your hearts. What man thinks important, God holds in contempt." It was the word *contempt* that blew me away. I found it difficult to believe the God who is love could hold such an emotion. But there it was, in black and white as it were. So how was I to respond?

Contempt is such a scary word. It conjures up in my mind the picture of someone looking at another with neither love nor hate, which are emotions that require caring, but with just contempt. Running into this scary word caused me to bounce back and look at two other words, *think* and *important*. "What man thinks important, God holds in contempt." I had to get all serious about what I thought important. The first thing I had to do was clarify my position. In so doing I came up with those things I *hold* as important and those things our materialistic society tries, with all its might, to convince me are important. I concluded it was the latter that God holds in contempt.

As so often happens, I found my answer beautifully expressed in the words of another. To live content with small means, to seek *elegance* rather than luxury, and *refinement* rather than fashion...to be *worthy*, not respectable and *wealthy*, not rich.... To study hard, think quietly, talk gently, act frankly.... To listen to stars and birds, babes and sages, with an *open heart*.... To bear all cheerfully, do all bravely, await occasions, hurry never. In a word, to let the spiritual, unbidden and unconscious, grow up through the common. This is to be my symphony (William Ellery Channing in *Earth Prayers*).

So much of what the world thinks important it portrays as absolutely necessary for us to *be* important. This is, of course, nothing more than screwed-up thinking. All we need remember are these words from *A Course in Miracles*. Engrave them on your heart and mind. "You are the work of God, and his work is wholly lovable and wholly loving. This is how a man must think of himself in his heart, because *this is* what *he is*."

# Birdbrain

It was the very first morning of the new year. Other than looking at the calendar, there was no way of verifying that fact by my actions; they were the same as last year. I was standing at the kitchen counter poised to place some bread in the toaster. My eyes wandered out the window and came upon some movement in the middle of the naked Bridal Wreath bush just below the window. There, perched on a branch was a rather plump sparrow. I had just checked the temperature in the back window, and it registered 20 degrees, and that's always a bit higher than the official temperature. The wind was out of the north, and a very light snow was falling. The wind chill, I'm sure, was below zero. Upon getting out of bed, I had set our thermostat on 70 degrees. My first reaction was to feel sorry for this little creature of God. The sparrow, however, didn't seem at all uncomfortable or concerned. She just sat there watching the world go by, although on that day, at that hour, there wasn't much world going by.

As I am sometimes prone to do, I began to wonder who was the fortunate one, the sparrow or me? I was in a place at least 50 degrees warmer than she was and out of the wind. I was preparing to eat my usual satisfying breakfast. This sparrow did look as though she knows all the eating places in town, like Dora Bray's feeder on East 7th Street, which I, on occasion, have the privilege of restocking.

After wondering and watching for a time, I sat down for my morning quiet time. It took awhile, but I was able to find, in the Book I read on a regular basis, the passage in Matthew where it speaks of our feathered friends: "Look at the birds in the sky. They do not sow or reap; they gather nothing into barns. Yet your heavenly Father feeds them. Are you not more important than they? Which of you by worrying can add a moment to your life span?"

After reading this, I began to understand why I had this feeling, as I was watching the sparrow, that she was watching me out of the corner of her eye. The look bordered on a smug glance. She was completely content with her state in life, with complete confidence that she would be taken care of. Of course, being "content" and "confident" in an animal is called "instinct." Do we, as so-called "rational" animals, possess such an instinct?

If we don't, it might have something to do with the words of the Man born in a barn that come before the statement concerning our feathered friends. "Do not lay up for yourselves an earthly treasure. Moths and rust corrode; thieves break in and steal. Make it your practice instead to store up heavenly treasure, which neither moths nor rust corrode nor thieves break in and steal. Remember, where your treasure is, there your heart will be also." The heavenly treasure we must seek parallels the "instinct" possessed by the sparrow. It means being content with who we are and what we have at any given time and having complete confidence that we are and always will be taken care of.

*Each Day a New Beginning* puts it this way, "We get what we need, in the way of relationships, adventures, joys and sorrows, today and every day. Celebrating what we get and knowing there is good in it eases whatever trial we are undergoing. We are cared for, right now! We need not lament what we think we need. We do have what we need. We will always get what we need, when we need it."

Maybe being called a "birdbrain" isn't such a put-down after all. Maybe that's what that little sparrow was sent to teach me on the first day of the new year.

# Superficiality: The Curse of Our Age

"Superficiality is the curse of our age. The doctrine of instant satisfaction is a primary spiritual problem" (Richard J. Foster).

Commenting on these words of Mr. Foster, the author of the book of meditations entitled *Touchstones* remarks, "As we have reached for instant cures, one minute answers, and quick highs, we have developed lifestyles that *foreclosed deeper possibilities*. For instance, when we fail to stay and resolve conflicts in a relationship, we miss the joys of a renewed understanding...the quickest and most efficient answer isn't always the best."

We're not just "ficial," we are *super*ficial. (I know there is no such word as "ficial," at least not in my dictionary. I was just trying to be clever.) In contrast to our superficiality, however, the word "understanding" caught my eye in this quote. Standing under, giving support, holding up, foundation. It makes me think of the parable of the Man born in a barn about building houses and the choices one makes. The quickest and most efficient way might be to build your house on sand. No need to spend a lot of time searching for a solid rock, or mixing some concrete and water with the sand and going to all the trouble of forming a foundation. We simply don't have time to wait. Those familiar with the parable might remember what happens to such a house: "The rains fell, the torrents came, the winds blew and lashed against the house. It collapsed under all of this and was completely ruined." The one solidly built on rock survived it all. It's important to note that nowhere will you find the promise that if we live good lives we will be spared the rains, torrents and winds that, if not prepared for, can completely ruin us. What we are promised is the means to survive and to be better people for the experience.

Returning to the commentary in *Touchstones*:

> Today our greatest temptation may be to grab for the fast solutions rather than allowing time for small but important steps to occur. When frustrated, it will help

to remember the difficulty may lie in our insistence on a quick answer. Sometimes simply being true to ourselves and standing as a witness while the answer develops are all that is asked of us.

That reminds me so much of the advice of the Native American elder to the children when lost in the woods: "Stand still!"

As I finished the last paragraph, and as if on cue, Fluffy, our cat, jumped up in my lap and demanded some "quality time." As I do most of my composing in a recliner, my laptop being a legal pad and a ballpoint pen, this just wasn't going to work. The quick solution would have been immediate expulsion in a gentle way. Being true to myself, however, I simply couldn't do that. So we spent the next ten minutes enjoying quality time together. It turned out to be the best interruption that could have happened — we both ended up purring. Relaxed and renewed, my work progressed.

There is a story in Zen circles about a man and a horse. The horse is galloping quickly, and it appears that the man on the horse is going somewhere important. Another man standing alongside the road shouts, "Where are you going?" The first man replies, "I don't know! Ask the horse!" Does this story strike a chord? Could it be that superficiality is a natural result of the pace of our lives? To help you find out, try simply standing still, being true to yourself, and allow the answer time to develop.

# Competition: The Root of All Evil

More and more I'm feeling that competition may be the "root of all evil." My dictionary defines competition as "the contention of two or more for the same object or for superiority; rivalry." The two words that most disturb me are "contention" and "superiority." Going back to the dictionary, contention is defined as "the act of contending; strife; conflict; struggle; dispute."

Of course, I realize that implying there is anything wrong with competition, let alone suggesting it is intrinsically evil, is tantamount to attacking a sacred cow. It is not a subject I take lightly. Competition has become such an integral part of our everyday existence that it is almost impossible to visualize what our lives would be like without it. Practically from the moment we're born to the moment we depart this life we are thrust into the competitive arena. Both baby clothes and caskets separate us.

What are the arguments for competition? It pushes us to strive to be our very best. Competition in manufacturing and commerce has sparked improvements in our way of life. These are strong arguments as long as we believe that the way things are is the best we can hope for. My problem is that I refuse to believe that assessment to be the case.

Is it really necessary to prove myself better than others in order to be my very best? Are we so lacking in imaginative wisdom that the only motivation we can think of to bring out the best in people is competition (strife, conflict, struggle, dispute)?

Where did we get these ideas? The Book I read on a regular basis records the evils of competition very early, in the story of Cain and Abel. Throughout all the Old Testament there are stories of strife, conflict, struggle and dispute, and I believe in most cases it had to do with competition. Then came the Man born in a barn, the One so many of us aim to follow. Speaking of baby clothes and caskets, he came into the world and departed it wrapped in swaddling clothes. Throughout the whole of his life I can't recall ever reading where he advocated competition as a good, let alone a virtue.

His concept of superiority is so contrary to our society's concept; the word "alien" comes to mind in reference to his attitude. On one occasion his closest followers were caught arguing about which of them was the most important. "So he sat down and called the twelve around him and said, 'If anyone wishes to rank first, he must remain the last one of all and the servant of all'" What A bummer!! I found it interesting that he didn't just say, "Okay, you guys, knock it off; enough of this superiority talk." He sat down and looked them straight in the eye. He felt the message was important enough to demand their full attention. The only competition he calls us to participate in is, "Be compassionate, as your Father is compassionate. Do not judge, and you will not be judged. Do not condemn, and you will not be condemned. Pardon, and you shall be pardoned. Give, and it shall be given to you. Good measure pressed down, shaken together, running over, will they pour into the fold of your garment. For the measure you measure with will be measured back to you."

My reading leads me to believe the only competition the Man born in a barn was interested in promoting was in the area of *most* loving, *most* tolerant, *most* in tune with the needs of others, *most* concerned with the feelings of others. What a bummer!!

# Minding Our Own Business

"This world would be a much better place if everybody would just mind their own business," he/she/they said.

On the street I saw a small girl, cold and shivering, in a thin dress, with little hope of a decent meal. I became angry and said to God, "Why did you permit this? Why don't you do something about it?" For a while God said nothing. That night he replied quite suddenly, "I certainly did something about it. I made you" (Source unknown).

When it comes to stories I use, this is a classic you'll probably remember. Charlie Brown's sister Sally had just been born. Charlie is naturally concerned with the world in which she will grow up. He expresses this concern to Linus, who listens intently with his thumb in his mouth and his security blanket against his ear. At a pause in Charlie's condemnation of world conditions, Linus interjects, "I think the world is better today than it was five years ago." This only adds fuel to the fire, as Charlie comes back with, "How can you say the world is better today? Don't you read the papers? Don't you watch TV? What makes you think the world is better today?" Linus says simply, "*I'm in it now.*"

Just what is the business we need to mind? It was not said of the Man born in a barn, "He went about minding his own business." Rather, it was said, "He went about doing good." He referred to himself as *the* Way, and he asked those who chose to follow him to be like "salt for the earth" and "light for the world." His message was simple, "Act in such a way as to make the world that your life directly affects better today than yesterday." That is the business we need to mind, and the world would be better if we all did that.

If I am to tend to my business of being salt for the earth, my shaker can only cover where I walk. As for being light for the world, my light is limited by space. I have one question for myself at the end of each day: "Is the world (at least the space I occupy) better because *I'm in it now?*"

~ 7 ~

Spirituality: An Equal
Opportunity Employer

# Spirituality: An Equal Opportunity Employer

We have a tendency to believe that *true* spirituality is reserved for the professionals, those who have made it their full-time job. These people are given special recognition and are held in high esteem. They are given titles and sometimes special uniforms or other garb. All of this tends to set them apart. They represent the ideal toward which we all must strive but know ahead of time we'll never make it.

Author Jack Kornfield spent six years in a Buddhist Monastery. He told of how lay people would come to the monastery, when they could, to attend services. They had fields to plow, children to raise and homes to tend. But they came in a devoted way. They meditated and they took the practice of awareness and loving-kindness to heart. The leader of the monastery would, at times, look around and say, "You monks are doing okay, spending all this time studying and meditating. But you want to know who's really accomplished something in this monastery? Look back there at those old men and those old women who are sitting there!" The monks would look back and realize the truth of what he had said.

Kornfield told this story in response to this question. "You were a monk for six years, and now you are offering these teachings to laypeople in America. Most people haven't had this kind of foundation. Is it really possible for the rest of us to go deeply into the spiritual life?" It's obvious the questioner was doubtful that one should dare to put an ordinary layperson on a par with a spiritual professional.

Did God intend this separation? Isn't spirituality as individual as fingerprints? An incident in the Book I read on a regular basis has always bothered me. After the death of the Man born in a barn, the growing community of believers is faced with a dilemma. A certain group of widows is concerned that they were being shorted in the daily distribution of food. The community leaders gather and come up with a solution. They conclude, "It is not right for us to neglect the Word of God in order to wait on tables. Look around among your own number, brothers, for seven men acknowledged to be deeply spiritual and prudent, and we shall appoint them to this task. This will permit us to concentrate on prayer and the ministry of the Word" (Acts 6: 1-4).

It seems to me the leaders had already forgotten a lesson taught by the Man born in the barn at the last meal they shared together. Would his taking the time to wash the feet of the apostles be classified as neglecting the Word of God? Was it not, rather, tangible evidence of how God wants his Word lived? He didn't give them a choice; he told them, "What I have done, you *must* do for one another." The problem I have with the decision of the community leaders is, I do not see waiting on tables as necessarily neglecting the Word of God.

The leaders of the early church had already set themselves apart. They were not part of the "your own number" crowd. I'll give them credit for seeking "deeply spiritual and prudent" table waiters, but it seems implied that they would still be considered less than those who "concentrate on prayer and the ministry of the Word."

We've spoken in this book about passionate desires. One of mine is that someday we might see and treat all people as equals. That we may someday recognize that a table waiter can be just as, or maybe more, deeply spiritual as anyone who may be classified as professional in the field.

# Doing Dishes – Seeking Wisdom

Let's begin with two short stories from the book *Taking Flight*.

A man asked a great mystic in the East to take him on as a disciple. "If you seek truth," said the mystic, "there are requirements to be fulfilled and duties to be discharged." "What are these?" asked the man. "You will have to draw water and chop wood and do the housekeeping and cooking." "I am in search of truth, not employment," said the man as he walked away.

Soon after the death of Rabbi Mokshe a man asked one of his disciples, "What did your teacher give the most importance to?" The disciple gave it a moment's reflection, then said, "To whatever he happened to be doing at the moment."

I was attracted to these stories because of a practice I began some time ago. It happened I was doing the dishes, by myself, after the evening meal. It was my turn. With just the two of us, there weren't many to do, but I really wasn't in the mood. It is, however, one of those duties that doesn't go away if you put it off. It only becomes more time-consuming for you or someone else the next time you tackle it. As I was reluctantly performing this duty, a question came to mind: Is there something that I could or should be doing at this moment that would be of more value to humankind and more beneficial to my well-being? Surprisingly, the answer came quickly and forcefully. It was NO! In my search for truth, this was my requirement that needed to be fulfilled, my duty to be discharged. I have found, because I am not a fast worker, that it takes about 20 minutes to do the dishes and straighten up the kitchen. The choice is mine, 20 minutes of drudgery, or a 20-minute search for truth.

Try it sometime. I think you will find the experience quite interesting. Pick an activity you find particularly boring, and in the midst of that activity ask yourself the question I posed.

Rephrase it, make it more personal but, above all, be honest in answering it.

These stories reminded me of the encounter between the rich young man and the Man born in a barn. The young man asked what he must do to be saved. The answer he received, as I read it, was to live his life to the full. Fulfill the requirements your life demands and discharge the duties that you have been assigned to do because of who you are. I was also reminded of the parable depicting the final judgment. The chosen were surprised because they were given credit for deeds they obviously didn't think were out of the ordinary. Their question was, "When did we do these things?" The response, in effect, was: When you made *most important* that which you were doing at the moment.

Linus, of *Peanuts* fame, coined the phrase, "There is no heavier burden than a great potential!" We constantly place this burden on ourselves and our children. The implication is that we are destined to be someone other than who we are. If I give the *greatest importance* to that which I happen to be doing at the moment, I will be living up to my full potential. Thoughts of future glory or happiness or regrets for past mistakes distract us from our only opportunity to make a real difference *now*, to learn from *this moment's* experiment in living.

# The Questioning Machine

The following is the message you will hear if you call a particular mental health professional when he is not home: "This is not an answering machine. This is a questioning machine. What it wants to know is, 'Who are you?' and 'What do you want?' two questions many people go through their whole lives never answering."

It sometimes seems that life, as we experience it today, is intent on keeping us from knowing who we are and what we really want. Our present society fills our lives with things and events that constantly distract us from the true meaning of life. I have made bold in this book to suggest that a little solitude might help.

My intense desire to wake us up to this fact is born out of my work with people in nursing homes. I've heard people say they don't like to visit nursing homes because they are so depressing. I'd like to suggest that it's just these people who would benefit the most from a visit. I say "benefit" only if they were to grapple with the question of why it depresses them; only if they were to eventually accept that aging is inevitable but need not be debilitating.

Some who study and work with the elderly say that many of the so-called mental disorders among this group are not a result of the natural aging process but are the way the elderly cope with the hostile environment in which they perceive themselves. They see the environment as hostile because they feel that they are losing control and that many of the things they took for granted are being taken from them.

Recently I overheard this statement from a couple in the hallway of the nursing home where I work. They had come for a visit and found the resident asleep, "We'll just let him sleep. He will benefit more from sleeping than our visit." I wanted to stand in their way, turn them around and send them back to that room. If nursing home residents benefited more from sleeping than a visit from friends, they would be the healthiest and happiest people in the world.

Loss of mobility is one of the greatest losses of aging. The elderly need visitors since they can no longer go out and visit others. If you've ever felt lonely in the midst of a crowd, then you have experienced an everyday occurrence among nursing home residents.

When we are young, we are often asked, 'What do you want to be when you grow up?" The proper answer should be, "I want to be me." The intended question was, "What do you want to *do* when you grow up?" It may only seem like a play on words, but understanding the difference may help us experience a healthy and happy old age. The philosopher Linus of *Peanuts* fame answered the question of what he wanted to be by simply saying, "Outrageously happy."

We live in a society that identifies who we are with what we do. Because of this unfortunate fact, I have found many among the elderly who feel that since they can no longer *do* they no longer care to *be*.

To avoid this feeling in our old age we need to begin *now* to learn how to *be* in the midst of our *doing*. And that word solitude comes back to haunt us. A saint of many centuries ago said, "Without solitude there can be no real people.... The measure of your solitude is the measure of your capacity for communion." In other words, until you're comfortable being yourself, your being with others will be less than completely satisfying.

Come on now, let's be honest: Who are you? and What do you want?

# Native American Traditions

As we reflect on the nature of spirituality, some Native American traditions come to mind.

In an old Navajo tradition a child's "Laugh Day" assumed even more prominence than his or her birthday, because it was on Laugh Day that a child is seen to respond to life with unconstrained joy. The parents had been awaiting the event with anticipation, and the person who first caused the baby to laugh became a godparent, assuming a special relationship with the child. It was from this point in time that the child's development in faith would later be traced. Laughter was thus conceived as that which brought into being the spiritual life.

According to an old Apache myth, Hactein, the high god, first created all sorts of animals and laughed uproariously at their shapes and funny behavior. Then Hactein made man and spoke to him, saying, "Laugh." The man laughed, and his laughter caused the dog to jump and wag his tail. His laughter caused the birds to break into singing. His laughter helped complete all that the god had initially brought into being at creation.

Finally the man was caused to fall asleep, and he dreamed of a creature like himself, but a woman. When he awoke and found her more than a dream, he began to laugh, and she laughed too. They laughed and laughed together. And that was the beginning of the world.

As I was reading these delightful traditions, I was reminded of my first introduction to Native Americans. Cowboy and Indian movies were quite popular in my youth, and the Indians were most often referred to as "savages." Somehow that image doesn't fit into the traditions just described.

"Laughter was thus conceived as that which brought into being the spiritual life." I like that idea. Maybe it's because it's so contrary to the way spirituality was presented as I was growing up. Anything that had to do with God or religion or the church was very serious business. To laugh in church was tantamount to slapping God in the face. What a bummer to find out that God has been laughing all along.

I think it was G.K. Chesterton who said he thought when the Man born in a barn went off by himself to pray he spent part of that time "roaring with divine laughter." I believe the following prayer is attributed to Saint Therese of Lisieux, "From silly devotions and sour faced saints, deliver us, O Lord!"

If I remember correctly, I believe my popularity as a public speaker increased in direct proportion to the number of *Peanuts* stories I used in my text. I also remember that my preparation time was much more fun.

The healing power of laughter, even in the physical realm, has been scientifically documented. These facts seem to affirm the truth contained in the Native American traditions that God made us to laugh. It's our ability to laugh that separates us from all the other animals in God's creation.

Unfortunately, like imagination and several other things, TV tends to rob us of laughter; the "laugh track" lets others do it for us. Laughter, to be effective, should be heard and felt in the gut. I wish they would install a control on TVs allowing us to shut off the laugh track so we can hear only the content of the program.

As the saying goes, "We come into this world crying while everyone around us is smiling. May we live in such a way that when we depart this world we will be smiling while everyone around us is crying."

# Behind Schedule

In this reflection I feel somewhat akin to a mosquito in a nudist camp: Where do I begin?

Don't you just hate it when you read something, and intellectually you know its true, but in your heart you wish it wasn't? That was my reaction when I read, "Our spiritual task is to become less rigid in our attachments and more accepting of the flow of life" (*Touchstones*). Hey, I'm an attached sort of guy. I especially like my daily routine; upset it, and I sometimes get ugly.

This brings me back to "The Criteria of Emotional Maturity." Number one was, "The ability to deal constructively with reality." Number two is "The capacity to adapt to change." The reason I am so taken up with these criteria is that I am hoping someday before I die I will be able to go through them and know that I have made each of them a part of my life. I know that when I can say "yes" to each of them, I will not only be emotionally mature but also will be spiritually mature.

This is especially important to me because, although I joke about it, I actually feel I'm running about 20 years behind schedule. A saint of many centuries ago proclaimed, "The glory of God is man/woman fully alive." I want to be *fully alive* before I die.

At the risk of incurring the wrath of my male friends, I must say that this maturity thing is much harder for us guys than for women. We have so much to unlearn surrounding the male stereotype. It's kind of embarrassing at times, but when I catch myself, it's rather humorous how I react to my wife's questions. When she asks me a question about almost anything, I automatically come up with words, none of which are, "I don't know." It's as though it would be a crime to admit I don't know everything. The question is asked, and I am off and running. If I am willing to stop in mid course and determine which direction

I am running, I often have to laugh. The answer is quite often coming from a male ego afraid to admit that he is not all-knowing.

Of course, I had help coming to this realization from one who loved me enough to point it out. A loving marriage can be a real boost to emotional maturity.

A number of years ago when I lived in another part of the country, I became acquainted with a group called "Emotions Anonymous." They use the twelve steps of A.A., adapting them to the emotions. Their first step is, "We admit we are powerless over our emotions, that our lives have become unmanageable." They go on to point out that even though we can't control our emotions we are not helpless in the face of them. We have a choice as to how we are going to react to them.

This encounter was a big boost to my emotional maturity. It freed me up from the notion that someday I will no longer be surprised by emotions that I would rather not experience. In other words, someday I'll be able to control my emotions — No Way!

I still read E.A. material daily and have often felt that a local chapter would be a good thing. I'm sure it would help me grow in "the capacity to adapt to change." Robert Louis Stevenson put it quaintly, "Sit loosely in the saddle of life." This gives us a good image of detachment. Detachment doesn't mean we stop caring. It means we have an inner wisdom telling us what we can control and what we cannot.

So the next time you hear a mosquito buzzing around your head, may it remind you to think of emotional/spiritual maturity.

# Living Simply

A man named Paul wrote these words to one of his students named Timothy, "We brought nothing into this world, nor have we the power to take anything out. If we have food and clothing, we have all we need.... The love of money is the root of all evil.... Man of God that you are, flee from all this. Instead, seek after integrity, piety, faith, love, steadfastness and a gentle spirit."

Frank Lloyd Wright, the great American architect, wrote, "As we live and as we are, Simplicity — with a capital "S" — is difficult to comprehend today. We are no longer truly Simple. We no longer live in simple terms or place. Life is a more complex struggle now. It is now valiant to be simple; a courageous thing to even want to be simple. It's a spiritual thing to comprehend what simplicity means."

Since a great number in our society today, whether they like it or not, are being forced to live a simpler lifestyle, it is not surprising to me that the word "simplify" is becoming a buzzword in the advertising world.

One of the most obvious, at the present time, is the ad for a particular automobile. Poor Bob, his only escape from a world gone mad is the simple sanity of his automobile. The word is also being used to hook us into buying any number of electronic gadgets that promise, of course, to simplify our lives.

Simplicity is not what I experience when I am faced with the price stickers on these autos and gadgets. Neither do I experience it when paying for repairs on such items after purchased.

Advertisers, many, many years ago, stopped selling products. They now sell security, happiness, contentment, confidence, power, excitement, dreams — and I'm sure you could add more. Above all, they plant seeds, instill ideas and turn completely unnecessary products into absolute needs. They attempt, and often succeed, in tying our self-esteem to the ownership of material things.

I remember seeing a powerful little film on this subject. A little girl sees a beautiful doll on the top shelf in a shop and decides she must have it. After much begging, the parents finally give her the money, and she runs to the store. The shop owner gives her the doll, which is almost as big as the little girl. A funny thing happens, however, as she runs home. With every step, the doll shrinks a little. By the time she reaches home the doll isn't nearly as desirable as it was when it was out of reach. I wonder how many of us have actually had such an experience.

Simplicity has not been the "in" thing because we have been brainwashed into believing that there is no way in H-E-double L we can be truly happy living ordinary lives. We have been forewarned that living simply is a complete bore.

Those who have bought into this couldn't possibly understand this statement from *Touchstones*, a book of daily meditations for men: "An important part of our lives is simply tending to our basic needs: sitting down daily to share a meal with loved ones, getting enough sleep, setting aside time for good grooming, spending leisure time with friends. We find balance in the basics." May I be so bold as to say that doing these things will do much more for one's self-esteem than owning any material thing.

"It's a spiritual thing to comprehend what simplicity means." In other words, it's a state of mind, not simply an external lifestyle. I believe firmly that in the near future, since each of us depends on a finite source of natural resources, we may all need to reexamine our lifestyles, as Gandhi said, "to live simply, so that others may simply live."

# A Monumental Bore

A pious old man prayed five times a day, while his business partner never set foot in church. And, now, on his eightieth birthday he prayed thus: "O Lord our God, since I was a youth, not a day have I allowed to pass without coming to church in the morning and saying my prayers at the five specified times. Not a single move, not one decision, important or trifling, did I make without first invoking your name. And now, in my old age, I have doubled my exercises of piety and pray to you ceaselessly night and day. Yet here I am, poor as a church mouse. But look at my business partner. He drinks and gambles and, even at his advanced age, consorts with women of questionable character, yet he's rolling in wealth. I wonder if a single prayer has ever crossed his lips. Now, Lord, I do not ask that he be punished; that would be unchristian. But please tell me: Why, why, why have you let him prosper, and why do you treat me thus?"

"Because," said God in reply, "you are such a monumental bore" (*Taking Flight* by Anthony de Mello).

Maybe it was because his prayer was a monologue instead of a dialogue. Maybe he didn't allow God to get a word in edgewise. Maybe his prayer consisted mainly in a set of instructions given to God on how God should act on his behalf. Words are meaningless if they are not the product of a pregnant silence. Father de Mello, commenting on this story, remarked, "The rule in a monastery was not 'Do not speak,' but 'Do not speak unless you can improve on the silence.' Might not the same be said of prayer?"

It's a personal thing, but the description "monumental bore" made me think of all the talk shows on TV and all the call-in radio shows. We seem intent on perpetuating the crime of talking things to death. There is a news event, and rather than allowing it to speak for itself we have to listen to a panel of experts who most often do little "to improve on the silence." Even sporting events are analyzed to death. The coach whose team is down by 40 points at the half has a mike thrust in front of his face so he can come up with a profound, "We didn't play very well."

In such an environment words tend to lose their true meaning, certainly their impact. Recently, I received a letter that said, "With this invitation, you've suddenly been elevated to a level of importance you are going to find exceptionally rewarding and quite unusual." The invitation was to a "private preview sale" at a furniture store in another city. They were right; I found the invitation "quite unusual." I suppose I should have sent them a thank you note, but for several days I felt so light-headed at the new level of importance to which I was elevated I couldn't get anything accomplished.

Turning from the ridiculous to the sublime, there is a beautiful poem by Pablo Neruda found in the book *Earth Prayers*:

And now we will count to twelve and we will keep still. For once on the face of the earth, let's not speak any language, let's stop for a second and not move our arms so much. It would be an exotic moment without rush, without engines, we would all be together in a sudden strangeness.... If we were not so singleminded about keeping our lives moving, and for once could do nothing, perhaps a huge silence might interrupt this sadness of never understanding ourselves and of threatening ourselves with death. Perhaps the earth can teach us as when everything seems dead later proves to be alive. Now I'll count to twelve, and you keep quiet and I will go.

Besides helping us "all be together," such silence never bores God.

# Wisdom: Learning to Listen to Life

Charlie Brown once observed that Linus would probably have to go to school longer than other children. The first part of his education would consist of unlearning what his sister Lucy taught him.

This is the way I feel about the latter part of my life. I've spent some time unlearning. This is true especially in the area of religion and spirituality.

In this book we've talked about the relative importance of the physical and spiritual, the worldly and the otherworldly. Their relative importance is really a moot point. The point is not whether we are spiritual or physical — we are both — but, rather, what we are doing with our lives.

One thing I unlearned is the idea that people are incapable of making right decisions for themselves without the help of religion. Another thing I unlearned is the belief that there is a direct connection between one's goodness and the time one spends in church. I believe it was Anthony de Mello, S.J. who observed, "Experience shows, alas, that our religious conviction bears as much relation to our personal holiness as a man's dinner jacket to his digestion." Think on that one.

What has helped me to unlearn is the practice of reading with a blank mind. A "blank" mind is more than an "open" mind. An open mind still allows us to hold on to preconceived ideas and compare them with new ideas, hopefully in a nonjudgmental way. A "blank" mind allows new knowledge to be poured into our minds without being filtered through preconceived notions. Our slate has been wiped clean, and it is ready to receive whatever will be written on it. I find this state of mind to be particularly important when reading something with which I am familiar, such as the Book I read on a regular basis.

At a recent gathering a speaker said, "The only thing we need fear is that which we do not know." True knowledge is our source of strength and power. It is not knowledge we need fear but our abuse of it. The knowledge of how to build a bomb never killed anyone. What has been done with that knowledge certainly has.

Wisdom is what we seek, and it is not the result of many years of education. Nor is it the result of many years of experience. These certainly can be contributing factors, but wisdom is something more. Wisdom is learning to listen to life. Wisdom teaches us to live in the real world, right where we now exist, and that's probably the most difficult thing each of us faces.

When reality becomes almost unbearable, wisdom may tell us to stop for a time and put our lives in perspective through meditation. To paraphrase an old song, "Wisdom is knowing when to hold and when to fold."

Most importantly, each and every one of us has equal access to this gift of wisdom. It has very little to do with education or age or religion, but it has everything to do with our happiness and contentment in this meantime.

Recently I became aware of a "far out" artist named Richard Stine. Quite likely you will hear more from him, but for this time let this quotation from him suffice:

> To tell you the truth I have a little voice in me that tells me what to do, what color to use, what pencil to pick up, what buttons to push. As long as I listen to that voice, I'm happy, even if the work I am doing ends up in the trash, which it does lots of the time. Sometimes the voice is not there, but I don't worry much, I work anyway. Then somehow it comes back, and I go bursting out again. All I know is that I'm happy when I'm in tune with it and miserable when I'm not.

That voice is wisdom. Listen to it!

# Stand Still and Listen

One of the most beautiful poems I have ever been privileged to know is from the Native American tradition. It's one I've referred to elsewhere in this book (see p. 96) and is simply titled "Lost." The poem was composed by an elder as a way of teaching children what to do if ever they were to find themselves lost in the forest.

The poem goes like this:

Stand still,
   the trees ahead and the bushes beside you are not lost.
Wherever you are is called *here*
   and you must treat it as a powerful stranger,
   must ask permission to know it and be known.
The forest breathes, *listen* it answers,
   "I have made this place around you.
   If you leave it, you may come back again saying, *here*.
   No two trees are the same to raven.
   No two branches are the same to wren.
   If what a tree or a bush does is lost on you,
      you are surely lost."
Stand still, the forest knows where you are,
   you must let it find you.

How different this beautiful expression of oneness with nature is from the TV commercial for a cellular phone: A slightly dazed adult leader announces to his troop of young Boy Scouts, "I think we're lost." One of the young scouts reaches into his knapsack, pulls out a cellular phone and hands it to the leader. The leader commends the young scout for following the motto of the scouts, "Be prepared."

My response to that commercial is to feel sorry for those scouts. As the poem says, "If what a tree or a bush does is lost on you, you are surely lost." Their chance for a truly spiritual experience was stymied by a cellular phone.

Persons in search of conscious contact with a Higher Power (God) can simply *stand still* and open their eyes and ears to creation. Forcing a spiritual experience is mostly wasted effort. Learning theology doesn't create a spiritual experience either. We only need to see and hear what is around us. This is a vast and marvelous universe, and it speaks for itself. It has always been there, and when we are ready to receive the message, we will" (*Touchstones*).

Or, as the elder says, "*The Forest Breathes, Listen.*"

It's my hang-up, I know, but it bugs me to see people walking and jogging out-of-doors with a Walkman plugged into their ears. "We only need see and hear what is around us." We seem never to be quite comfortable doing what we are doing, or being where we are. I remember camping several years ago in a heavily wooded campground just outside of Cincinnati, Ohio. I spent two quiet days and nights; then the weekend arrived. The wooded area was invaded and became as noisy as any city. Listening to the forest became impossible.

This whole cellular phone incident is a parable on how we have treated our relationship to God. Rather than seeing and recognizing God in everything and everyone around us, He/She is someone we must contact. Thank goodness there is a toll-free 800 number available.

"If what a tree or bush does is lost on you, you are surely lost." What do trees and bushes do? Obviously, what they do is of no consequence if they happen to occupy space where we have decided to build a road or erect a structure.

How arrogant we have become! God has placed us in a beautiful garden that we might tend it. Just like the first time, we are once again failing to heed God's warnings. On what snake will we blame our failings this time?

# Discernment

Age doesn't automatically bring about wisdom. In the case of Fred, we have an example of how it can.

Fred was advanced in years and lived alone. His small apartment, in a large city, overlooked a vacant lot. From the second floor he could see trees and grass, and he loved to listen to the song of the birds.

One day this serenity was shattered by five boys who decided to use the lot as a playground. They were boisterous and extremely loud. They always seemed to show up at Fred's naptime.

This turn of events upset Fred, for he wasn't sure what recourse he might have. He did not own the lot, and the boys were not doing anything wrong. It was obvious the boys had found their place to play, and Fred's naptime was of no concern to them.

Fred's mind, fine-tuned from many years of problem solving, searched for a solution. He wasn't about to give into self-pity. One day he opened up his window and invited the boys up for a cold drink at the end of their play time. The boys accepted his invitation. While they were with him, Fred told the boys how much he appreciated their loud play, telling them it reminded him of his own youth. He said to reward them he was going to give each of them 50¢ each day they came to play. The boys agreed to that arrangement enthusiastically.

On the third day after the arrangement began, Fred had bad news for the boys. He had had some unexpected expenses, so on that day he could only offer them 25¢. He also told them there may be days when he may not be able to afford even that much.

The boys grudgingly accepted the 25¢. Fred overheard them in the hallway as they were leaving, discussing whether they would be willing to do what they had been doing for a quarter or maybe for nothing. That was the last day Fred saw the boys.

I believe it was the Man born in a barn who commended resourcefulness and who urged his followers, in order to survive this world, to be innocent as doves and cunning as serpents. Somehow I think he would approve of Fred's actions.

Wisdom is defined in my dictionary as "1. The power of true and right discernment; conformity to the course of action dictated by such discernment. 2. Good practical judgment; common sense."

There is a word in that definition that isn't used much, but it is the key word. "Discernment" is not something that we gain simply by using our minds. It is not a conclusion we come to by following a certain mental formula. Discernment is the process in which we involve our whole being when faced with what life has to offer. Discernment requires the interaction of our minds and bodies, the physical and the spiritual, our hearts and souls and, last but not least, our gut. In fact, that might be the truest test, "How does it feel in the gut?"

The dictionary refers to "true and right discernment" as a "power," and so it is. This power, however, will be of very little value to us if we fail to take the next step and "conform to the course of action dictated by such discernment."

How we solve our problems is a good test of the wisdom we possess. Discernment helps us recognize, as our heart's wisdom tells us, that "life is an adventure to be lived, not a problem to be solved."

The boys undoubtedly found another playground to continue to live their adventure. Fred regained his time to remember peacefully the many adventures of his past, and they all lived happily ever after.

# God's Will

Part of our calling as members of the human community is to unconditionally love and support the people emotionally close to us. We have been drawn together for purposes wonderful but seldom readily apparent. We need one another's gifts, compassion, and inspiration in order to contribute our individual parts to the whole.

It would be difficult to come up with a better answer than the above to the question of what is God's will for us. As so often happens, we spend so much time looking for a profound answer, we look right past the simple one. Let me be quick to add, "simple" does not automatically mean "easy."

Think about it. If all of us adult persons were fully committed to "unconditional love and support" for the "people emotionally close" to us, what more would be needed? Unfortunately, the people emotionally close to us are often the ones to whom we give the least amount of unconditional love and support.

"When people bother you in any way, it is because their souls are trying to get your divine attention and/or blessing" (Catherine Ponder). I also believe that spiritual awakenings are sometimes disguised as rude awakenings.

Our opportunities to help and inspire those emotionally close to us abound and will be with us all of our lives. The problem is they are sometimes so seemingly insignificant they are easily missed.

Why this little story kept popping into my head as I was writing the above I'm not sure, but I decided not to ignore it: This couple went to see a marriage counselor for help. Each was accusing the other of making all the decisions. The counselor encouraged them to sit down and list the decisions that needed to be made and decide how to divide them up and which may need mutual attention. The very next session they were all smiles. When asked why, they said they had resolved their conflict and this was due to following the counselor's expert advice. When asked what compromise they had come to, the husband quickly answered, "We have decided that I will make all the major decisions and my wife the minor ones." Asked to explain further, he said, "She will have the say so as to where we are going to live, how our money will be spent, how to raise the kids, etc. On the other hand, I will have the say so with regard to major decisions such as what foreign policy the President should follow, what action would be most appropriate to defend against terrorists, whether to raise or lower income taxes, etc."

Maybe it came to mind because men seem to have trouble with issues emotionally close to them. They are more comfortable dealing with the so-called major issues. We pray in Psalm 40, "To do your will, O my God, is my delight, and your law is within my heart." The real major issues are "heart" issues not "head" issues.

Not only do we need to nurture and inspire others, but our personal development, emotionally and spiritually, demands that we honor ourselves in like fashion. Self-love, full self-acceptance is necessary before we can give anything of lasting value to someone else.

When we add all of this up, the bottom line is: There is no insignificant encounter in our passage through this life. Every meeting with someone else is part of the destiny of both parties. Their growth and ours is at stake. "We have been drawn together for purposes wonderful but seldom readily apparent."

"...you don't get to choose how you're going to die. Or when. You can only decide how you're going to live. Now" (Joan Baez).